CREATIVE
Miniatures

For my son Mark and all my students

'In the fields of observation, chance favours only the prepared mind.'
Louis Pasteur

CREATIVE
Miniatures

A Complete Guide
to Miniature Painting

PATRICIA MOY

BLITZ EDITIONS

Author Note
The caption for each photograph of a miniature contains the actual
dimensions of the work. However, in some cases, the works themselves
are not reproduced to full size.

CREATIVE MINIATURES

First published in Australasia in 1992 by
Simon & Schuster Australia
20 Barcoo Street, East Roseville NSW 2069

A Paramount Communications Company
Sydney   New York   London   Toronto   Tokyo   Singapore

Published by Blitz Editions
an imprint of
Bookmart Limited
Registered Number 2372865
Trading as Bookmart Limited
Desford Road
Enderby
Leicester
LE9 5AD

Designed by Anna Warren
Typeset in Australia by Asset Typesetting Pty Ltd
Printed in Hong Kong by South China Printing Company (1988) Limited

Cover photograph: Patricia Moy: 'Friday's Poppies'. Detail from a large
watercolour. In a private collection. Patricia Moy: 'Poppies'. Watercolour
on ivorine. In a private collection. Photograph by Jonathan Chester.

CONTENTS

INTRODUCTION

While gathering material for these discussions, a friend and artist, well known for her large contemporary work, made an interesting comment. She said she felt miniatures were like 'pillow talk with a lover'. It was exciting to think that miniatures could still stir the same emotions they did 500 years ago.

Lifted from the pages of the illuminated manuscript, where they had been used to instruct, the first limnings, as miniatures were called, were portraits made to delight royalty and act as a surrogate for a missing loved one.

The habit has never died. Teenagers today carry a photo of a special person in a wallet. It may be shown to a trusted friend; it's often kissed just before sleep ... Little has changed.

When Hans Holbein painted Ann of Cleves for Henry VIII, the King was so taken by the image that a marriage was arranged. History records that the lady did not match the image and divorce was swift.

Images have been made that were so precious that death could not part them from their owners. Richard Cosway painted Mrs Fitzherbert in 1790 for George IV, who wore the image constantly for 40 years, it's said, and requested it be buried with him.

The secret nature of the miniature has always been part of its charm. Partly because of the nature of the image, and partly because of the delicate quality of watercolour, miniatures were placed in lidded boxes and later, closed lockets. Even today, beautiful collections held by art galleries are rarely on display. Special permission must be gained to view them.

Yet miniatures are at last emerging from their long sleep, and are arousing public interest. There is a renaissance world wide. But the butterfly which is emerging from its cocoon differs, in many ways, from the parent which laid the egg. Common traits are still present: it is still small enough to hold in the hand; it still delights and intrigues; but it has emerged into a world which has changed, which is much more exciting and stimulating, and the new wings reflect this.

These pages are about the new reflections in the wings of the butterfly. Look closely and you will still see the parent. The family tree of miniature painting is examined and its roots exposed. Just like any family there will be members who carry on family traditions, and there will be others who are affected by their changing environment, and who wish to reflect it.

Many artists are working in exciting ways in miniature in Australia, and their voices have not been heard before. Without exception, these artists work in large format, but enjoy the change and the challenge of miniatures.

Yet, can there be such a thing as a contemporary miniature?

Phoebe Sholto Douglas, a member of the English Royal Society of Miniature Painters, Sculptors and Gravers (one of the most prestigious societies for traditional miniature art), made an interesting comment in an excellent series she wrote for the English magazine *The Artist*, in 1983. She wrote:

It is easy to condemn modern miniature painting on the ground that qualities, taste and execution of the former masters have been abandoned. This would be to deny that such a thing as change can be permitted in so personal a thing as portraiture. It would mean that convention, once established, was immutable for all time no matter what alterations there might be in the world in general.

She went on to speculate that in the seventeenth century there were, no doubt, those who were critical of the changes which took place, when realism crept in and elaborate ornamentation declined. She also said:

There will always be change — in manners, customs, clothes, hairstyles, furnishings — the whole way of life. The artists of the day will interpret and record these changes. This is not to say their techniques have declined.

I find myself agreeing with her.

To say that there can only be one way of painting miniatures is, in my opinion, akin to saying there can only be one way of painting and it must be in the style of Rubens or David or Ingres.

There are miniaturists who feel that a miniature is defined by technique, and size is secondary to that definition. They feel that this technique requires that no brush stroke be raised. Yet Nicholas Hilliard (1547–1619), renowned for his exquisite treatment of lace ruffs on the costume of the day, used 'a very full brush of white lead, virtually dribbling the paint onto the surface'. The shadow which fell from this thick paint helped the illusion of the fine lace ruff. He built up his famous 'jewels' on tiny mounds of turpentine resin over a burnished silver ground.

We all know what happened when the Impressionists displayed their first works. They were scorned and ridiculed. They threatened conservative society because they viewed art in a new way. Their paint was loose and freely applied and it followed, in many instances, the theory of visual colour mixing — not a new technique, having been used by miniaturist Peter Cross, in 1684. What a loss to the world it would have been if the critics had been successful!

The young director of a performance in 1990 of the famous *Oberammergau* passion play, was the recipient of severe criticism for the changes he made in the centuries-old play. His reply still rings in my ears: 'I want to leave the next generation the fire and not the ashes'.

I hope that by gathering together information about traditional techniques and exciting new methods, this book may serve as a gentle introduction to a beautiful art.

Possibilities which are explored here include the use of paper (black and white), ivorine, ivory piano keys, scraperboard and board as supports; the use of watercolour, gouache, ink, acrylic, oil and collage as possible mediums; and tracking down the source of inspiration for different artists, and watching how they express that inspiration. I hope these discussions may inspire you to find your own, very personal expressions.

These are the reflections in the new wings of the butterfly. I hope some of the ideas discussed may start a wind beneath your wings.

Patricia Moy, 1991

Part One

CHAPTER 1
A Brief History

How it all Began

Where did these exquisite little paintings come from? Miniatures came into existence from the detachment of the fixed painting within the text of the illuminated manuscript, becoming a portable item about 500 years ago. Though it is not possible to pinpoint the date exactly, the painting of the first detached miniature, or 'limning', as they were called, coincides with a sequence of events which took place in Europe during the fifteenth century.

In the ancient world, literature was an oral tradition and texts were read aloud. The decorations and embellishments came when it was considered that illustrations would aid understanding of the written word. Pictures were used to illuminate or throw light on a subject.

From the seventh to the twelfth century, books were a monastic production, and artist and scribe were the same person. This individuality disappeared with the emergence of the commercially produced book. Now, as Donald Jackson relates in *The Story of Writing*, many craftsmen were involved and they were organised by a 'Stationer' (a bookseller), who stayed in one place and co-ordinated the work. The scribe, 'he who illuminated the initials; he who made the pictures', and all those involved in the actual making of the book, had their separate jobs.

During the twelfth to the fifteenth century, many of the books produced were

Bibles, with the same set of religious pictures, colours and arrangement. A description of a 'Book of Hours', produced in France during the reign of Henry VII (1485–1509), gives a clear idea of what these books were like. It consisted of 77 leaves of vellum, each measuring 18 cm x 13 cm (7 in x 5 in) — an interesting measurement in view of later standards set for miniatures in some countries. Each page had an illuminated border. The borders were composed of flowers and fruit, interspersed with grotesque animals, birds and human figures, mostly eccentrically conceived. Both the capital letters and the borders were heightened with gold, sometimes flat and sometimes brilliantly burnished. There were 20 miniatures, some the size of the full page and some smaller.

In Germany in the mid 1400s, Johannes Gutenberg had developed movable type (the Chinese had invented it centuries before), and by 1500, there were more than 1000 print shops in Europe, and several million books had been printed. What rough winds of change must have swept through the atelier of the illuminator!

Meanwhile, there were developments in the style of art produced. The Renaissance, which had begun in Italy in 1300, and continued to 1600, reached France in the late 1400s. At this time artists began to make man and the heroic aspects of his past, rather than God, the centre of interest. Their creative images reflected this.

The scientific laws of perspective had been developed in Florence. Da Vinci, Michaelangelo and Raphael were leaving an indelible mark. Flemish artists had developed oil as a new medium. German artist, Albrecht Dürer, and later Hans Holbein, the younger, travelled to Italy to study the principles of Renaissance art. The techniques of both artists were to have a strong influence on later miniaturists.

The first detached limnings emerged in the context of all the above. In France in the early 1500s, Jean Clouet was a painter to the Valois court. Trained in the finely wrought techniques of the Burgundian illuminators, it is he who is credited with being the originator of the portrait miniature as a separate portable art.

In 1526, three miniatures (almost certainly by Jean Clouet) were sent to the Tudor court of Henry VIII. In two lockets, each elaborately decorated with a symbolic program, were portraits of Francis I and his two sons. The three works of art, since lost, caused a sensation at court, and may well have been the link between miniature painting within the manuscript and the now-portable portrait.

Early English Miniaturists

In England the art was to grow with great vitality. Between 1525 and 1526, Lucas Hornebolte, court painter to the Tudor court, had commenced a series of miniatures of Henry VIII. Hans Holbein followed Hornebolte as court painter, and produced some of the most beautiful portraits in the history of the art.

Possibly best known of all miniaturists is Nicholas Hilliard, who wrote an essay:

'A Treatise concerning the Arte of Limning' (*c.* 1600), which tells us so much about the joys and frustrations of miniature painting. Twenty years later, Edward Norgate wrote a more concise manuscript dealing with the practicalities of the art. Isaac Oliver, Samuel Cooper and many others were to follow during the seventeenth century, still using the same

William Wood (1764–1810). 'Clarissa' (Mrs Clara Dougan). Watercolour on ivory. Painted 1799. Image size 7.8 cm x 6.5 cm (3 in x 2½ in). In a private collection. Wood painted an original and two copies of 'Clarissa'. This portrait is thought to be either entry No. 5659 or 5667. Wood played a prominent part in forming the Society of Artists in Watercolour, and was its first president in 1808. He died two years later. His personal records of his paintings are held by the Victoria and Albert Museum, London.

methods as the illuminators: watercolour
and vellum.

In 1702, ivory was introduced to
England (possibly after the work of
Rosalba Carriera of Venice had been seen).
By 1720, very few miniaturists continued
to work on vellum. The conversion to
ivory was almost total.

Forty years later, Jeremiah Meyer was
credited with developing a technique of
painting on this difficult, slippery surface.

By the late 1700s the stunning works of
Richard Cosway, George Engleheart, John

Smart and William Wood dominated the
scene. The art was at its peak. It was the
rise before the fall.

A major and a minor development were
to cause its demise. The introduction of
photography, by 1840, was the major
cause, joined, to a lesser degree, by clients'
demands for larger work in the same
technique (a demand which was not
financially viable for the miniaturist).

It is interesting that, though the portrait
miniature appears to have come from the
work of Clouet in France, it had only fitful

A brief list of some important early English miniaturists

Born–Died	Artist	Sequence of Events
c. 1490/5–1544	Lucas Hornebolte	All work was called limnings, and was painted on
1497–1543	Hans Holbein	vellum or card.
?1483–1576	Levina Teerlinc	
1547–1619	Nicholas Hilliard	
–1617	Isaac Oliver	
c. 1590–1664	John Hoskins	In 1630, gessoed card replaced playing card as
?1608–1672	Samuel Cooper	secondary support.
?1609–?1660	Alexander Cooper	
?1605–1690	Richard Gibson	
c. 1645–1724	Peter Cross	First to use primary colour stipple–optical blend.
1682–1740	Bernard Lens III	First English artist to paint watercolour on ivory — perhaps after seeing the work of Rosalba Carriera of Venice (1675–1758).
1735–1789	Jeremiah Meyer	First to use ivory to its maximum potential.
1742–1810	Richard Crosse	Most miniatures were painted on ivory.
1742–1821	Richard Cosway	From 1760, miniatures were exhibited in public
1742/3–1811	John Smart	exhibitions, and some miniaturists became members
1752–1829	George Engleheart	of the Royal Academy.
1764–1810	William Wood	The size of the miniature continued to increase.
1777–1845	Andrew Robertson	These two artists helped to organise the Society of Artists in Watercolour.

Note: From 1880 on, women started to play a more active role. The Royal Society of
Miniature Painters, Sculptors and Gravers was established in 1895.

patronage in that country during the first 200 years. Some of the most brilliant work appears in France in the early nineteenth century. Isabey and Leon Larue (called Mansion, a pupil of Isabey), both produced some beautiful portraits. Mansion exhibited at the Royal Academy in London, but by now the work was quite large — 14.1 cm x 10.5 cm (5⅝ in x 4⅛ in), as was the fashion.

When one considers the tender nature of watercolour on ivory (watercolour fades if exposed to too much light for a long period, and ivory buckles and cracks if exposed to extremes of temperature), that it is still possible to see miniatures today which are 500 years old is surely a credit to their custodians.

The Silhouette

The origins of silhouette go back to classical antiquity, and there is evidence of its emergence at the end of the seventeenth century as an art form in Europe, but its heyday was through the eighteenth century and into the early years of the nineteenth century.

The publication of Johann Kasper Lavater's *Essays on Physiognomy* in the 1770s possibly did much to stimulate interest in silhouette, since the book was illustrated with this type of portrait.

After this publication, silhouettes became fashionable with admirers as diverse as the writer Johann von Goethe (who was himself a cutter), the Empress Catherine the Great of Russia, and King George III of England. In fact there is a famous painting of Princess Elizabeth, third daughter of George III, sitting by a window at Windsor Castle, engaged in her favourite hobby — cutting silhouettes.

Silhouette took its name from a French Minister of Finance, Etienne de Silhouette

(1709–1767). It was his hobby to cut profiles from black paper. A silhouette is an outline of an object against the light, commonly a profile portrait in black. The term usually refers to the side view of the head.

The earliest silhouettes were possibly cut from black paper with scissors, but the art is thought to have achieved its greatest heights with the painted silhouette, and these became the finest miniatures.

Original portraits were life size. The subject sat between a candle lamp and a glass screen, behind which was a sheet of oiled paper. The artist, working on the other side, drew around the life-size shadow on the paper. The outline was blacked in later, or cut out and backed with black material. This was called 'hollow cutting'.

In 1775 Mrs Samuel Harrington invented the pantograph — a mechanical device for enlarging or reducing drawings. This device meant that the artist could produce a copy of the original silhouette at any time. By the late 1700s it was advertised by one artist that he could produce '16 different sizes down to ¼ inch' (0.6 cm). These minute silhouettes were, no doubt, set in jewellery, since silhouettes of this size were painted on ivory and often used this way.

One of the greatest silhouettists was considered to be John Miers (1758–1821); Isabella Beetham (fl. 1750), who painted on the reverse side of glass, is thought to be at least his equal. 'Verre eglomise', the technique of painting on the back of glass using paint with gold and silver foils was also used.

At the end of the eighteenth century, silhouette went into a decline from which it was rescued by the efforts of a French refugee, Augustin Amant Constant Fidèle

Edouart (1789–1861). He was a freehand cutter who arrived in England in 1814. He is said to have initiated the second and last great period of the English silhouette. His output was enormous, and in 1835 he published a treatise on the subject (now extremely rare). Unfortunately, Edouart lost most of his collection of ten thousand duplicates in a shipwreck. Luckily many of the original silhouettes survived.

Most European countries have had silhouettists of some standing. Germany had the delicate lace cutwork of Christina Luise Duttenhofer (1776–1829) and Philippe Otto Runge (1776/7–1810).

William Alport (?–1831). Unknown Woman. Painted c. 1807. English. Painted on paper, silhouette. Inside-frame size 10.5 cm x 8 cm (4⅛ in x 3⅛ in). In the collection of Janet Niven.

In France, A. Forberger (1762–1865) and E. P. Sideau (fl. 1782), and in Austria, Leopold Gross (fl. 1790) and H. Loeschenkohl (fl. 1780) were well known.

Highlighting with bronze was pioneered at the close of the eighteenth century. Some silhouettes were painted on plaster using beer as a medium. Plaster was a common background, the whiteness giving maximum contrast to the sharpness of the 'shade', as silhouettes were sometimes called. These, however, were extremely fragile, and would crack on merest impact.

Silhouettes were often made when fashionable middle-class families went out for the day. These were full length and cost 'a shilling'. Information and advertising were placed at the back of the silhouette, just as was done with miniatures. They were sometimes framed in black papier-mâché, with a small gilt oval around the image. Examples still appear in beach resorts, and they have become one of the few collectables still available at a moderate cost.

SILHOUETTES IN AMERICA

The first recorded mention of silhouettes in America is in a letter by Harriet Pinckney, a southerner, written in 1799, and mentioning her 'shade' by Thomas Wollaston. The whereabouts of this profile are unknown.

In spite of its comparative brevity, the history of silhouettes in America is colourful. They grew in popularity during the early nineteenth century. Charles Willson Peale (1741–1827) was one of the most ingenious silhouette artists. He used a 'physionotrace' together with a stencil machine to 'produce a correct indented outline by any steady hand in a few moments'. He was a serious and excellent artist, who had been in succession and sometimes simultaneously, a saddler, clock maker, silversmith, taxidermist, soldier, legislator, educator and scientist (what lengths we artists have to go to to survive).

His nephew, Charles Peale Polk (1767–1822) made some of the rarest types of silhouettes in America: profiles on a gold background.

William Henry Brown (1808–1883) was a freehand cutter, whose style was pure and severe. He was an artist and a social observer, who produced the *Portrait Gallery of Distinguished American Citizens*, published in 1846. His silhouettes (full length) were shown along with lithographs and crayon drawings prepared by other artists.

Almost the entire edition of *Portrait Gallery* was destroyed by fire, so copies are extremely rare.

Also recorded are two armless silhouettists, who showed amazing ingenuity: Miss Honeywell, who cut with the scissors in her teeth, and Sanders K. G. Nellis, who used his toes.

As in other parts of the world, demand for silhouettes ceased when the daguerreotypes arrived in America after 1839.

Early Frames and Cases

When limnings first separated from the manuscript leaves, they were kept in tiny wooden or ivory boxes. A crystal (glass) was placed on top of the work and the box was made with a lid to prevent fading. These miniatures were circular in format, and continued in this shape until 1577, when Nicholas Hilliard suddenly evolved the oval as being the ideal shape for the portrait. The oval shape allowed a hand to be included, more of the costume to be

seen, and removed the image from that of the medal and coin.

A miniature painted by Levina Teerlinc (?1483–1576) had been worn as a jewelled locket as early as 1562, and it became increasingly popular to frame and wear them in this way.

As Hilliard was originally apprenticed to a jeweller and goldsmith, he naturally encased his miniatures, which he painted for Elizabeth I and James I, in the most elaborate cases.

Hilliard was not directly on the royal payroll until 1586, so, in search of new clients, he opened a shop in Gutter Lane, off Fleet Street, London in the early 1570s. No longer the treasure of the royal court, the miniature became available to anyone prepared to pay. This proved to be the democratisation of these small works.

Sometimes worn on a chain from the waist, they were mostly worn around the neck. The cases were now extremely elaborate, decorated with pearls, rubies and sardonyx, as was the Drake Jewel which Elizabeth I gave to Sir Francis Drake in 1586 or 1587. There are two copies of the miniature within this jewel which have survived — the first evidence of mass production of the art. To prevent fading, these lockets were still lidded, just as the boxes had been.

Ebony frames became popular by the end of the sixteenth century, and early in the seventeenth century, miniatures were framed in sets. Charles I had eight framed together. The work increased in size and migrated from the sleeping quarters where they had been kept in secret. Rectangular works became popular. They were hung on walls, but behind curtains for protection. They had become a collectable art form.

Some frames were made of bog oak, pinchbeck and steel, but increasingly fine

Reverse side of unknown miniature showing initials 'R.J.' Initials in seed pearls on plaited hair. It shows two pieces of hair — brown and blond — intertwined. Image size 6.3 cm x 5.2 cm (2½ in x 2 in)

gold frames were used in the style still seen today.

In the mid-eighteenth century, artistic hair arrangement became fashionable. Tiny locks of hair, arranged in fine designs by professional hair workers, were placed in the backs of the lockets which contained miniatures. Sometimes the hair would be that of the sitter depicted; but often the hair worker would use horse hair, which was much easier to manipulate.

As works became larger in the nineteenth century, frames became more elaborate and ornate. Papier-mâché frames were popular. These often had small acorn or floral hangers. They were extensively used for silhouettes at the peak of their popularity.

Original Materials, Supports and Techniques

Monks in the medieval monastery had the chemistry to make colours for illumination. The basic material was 'body colour', that is, colour to which white has been added causing it to be opaque (no longer transparent). Later, in miniature painting, there was a clear separation between the foundation of body colour, and the clear transparent washes which were floated over the top to complete the work.

The recipes of the miniature painters of the Elizabethan era vary little from the recipes for watercolour paints, first published in the nineteenth century. It would seem that for 300 years there had been little or no change.

Nicholas Hilliard (*c.* 1600) discussed grinding pigments in pure water, binding them with gum arabic, and making them less brittle by the addition of sugar candy. Other artists, writing at about the same time, suggested that, for difficult colours, the addition of white wine, alcohol or urine be used as wetting agents in addition to, or in place of, water.

This was not the only occasion where an artist put 'something of himself' into his work. Where watercolour was proving difficult to apply, ear wax would sometimes be used. This personal addition was not unique to English and European painting. The Chinese had previously discovered its beneficial use.

Early in the nineteenth century, sugar and honey were used to retain moisture in the watercolour cake. Later in the century, glycerine was used, because it acted in the same way.

As with the text of the illuminated manuscript, the choice of support for the early limnings was still vellum or parchment, the medium was watercolour, and the early works still bore gold work and calligraphy, almost as if they had been cut from the page.

Vellum is fine skin with the hair and flesh removed. It has a tendency to curl if overwet or affected by changes in the atmosphere. A support had to be found. Playing cards of the day were made to withstand much handling, just as they are today. They were made with cyphers on one side, but the backs were plain. They became the choice to be used as a backing support by the first miniaturists, as is evident on close inspection of the backs of these early miniatures. The vellum was cut to size and pasted, with a flour paste, to the plain side of the card. These pasted cards, or tablets as they were called, were then left to dry under pressure.

The pigments had to be ground by the artist — artist's colourmen (who ground pigments and mixed colours for the artists) were not to arrive until well into the eighteenth century. This meant that the artist was in control of the grade of his pigment; for instance white would be ground in three stages: the first would be kept to depict flesh, the finer grade for linen, and the finest for satin.

When the tablets were dry and ready to use, a light flesh colour called the 'carnation' would be mixed and swept across the surface of the tablet. This carnation was to later represent the lightest skin tone of the sitter, perhaps the light on cheeks and nose. Different carnation tones would be prepared so that a supply would be held ready to be matched to the individual sitter.

It took many years of training to work on vellum in this way. If the mixture was too wet, the vellum would curl. If too dry and thick, the mixture would later crack.

More than just the area for the skin would be covered with carnation, to be later washed away where it was not required. It was impossible to match or add. If working *ad vivum*, from the sitter, the artist would match the skin colour from his selection of carnation covered tablets and commence to paint in the darker tones in washes of red and grey.

The wonderful engravings of Albrecht Dürer (1471-1528) were known to these early artists, and his system of achieving tone by cross hatching was copied in paint. Some used a system of dots or stipple, and some used fine strokes which followed the form. These strokes were painted with an almost dry brush, so that the undersurface would not be disturbed and the vellum was never too wet. This was the method used by the early Burgundian illuminators, to be carried on by the makers of the first portable miniatures.

Contrary to the general belief, the brushes used then (and now) were not single hair brushes. They were larger brushes with a very fine point. It was (and still is) important that the brush have a good 'well' (the area between the tip and the metal ferrule). This can hold a quantity of paint, allowing the artist to make many fine strokes from the one dip.

Brushes were called 'pencils' and were handmade by the artist. The hair commonly used came from the tail of the squirrel. The hairs were collected, cut and shaped by hand. They were tied and inserted into the quills of waterfowl. These quills were then mounted on sticks of brasilwood or ivory.

Prior to the use of graphite, metal point was used during the Renaissance. It is quite possible that some miniatures were drawn first with silverpoint, which was used by the early scribes in their

The working desk or easel which was in use from 1525 to about 1850. It usually consisted of a box with drawers for colours and brushes, and a baize-covered hinged board at the top, which could be adjusted to various angles.

preparatory drawings for manuscripts. The palette was made of mother-of-pearl. Later it was replaced with an ivory palette.

Prepared pigments were placed in shells (much as shell gold was prepared until recently when, of course, the shell was replaced by a plastic cap). Later, prepared pigments were stored in turned ivory boxes.

Two water containers were used. One was to wash the brush and one in which to dip the brush before using fresh colour.

A good light which fell across the work from left to right, for the right-handed artist, was vital. This ensured no shadow would fall from the artist's hand.

The artist's work box and easel were one. It contained drawers for the storage of palette, paints and brushes. On the top of the box was a hinged board, which could be adjusted to different angles. The prepared tablet would be attached to this board before work commenced.

CHAPTER 2
Materials Today

In international competition for miniatures today, there is a category for every medium in two- and three-dimensional work.

The following are the categories offered by the Del Bello Gallery, Toronto, Canada, for its Fifth Annual International Exhibition of Miniature Art, in 1990:

Paintings, Sculptures and Bas-relief, Graphics, Computer Art, Printmaking, Watercolours, Drawings, Pastels, Coloured Pencils, Scrimshaw, Photography, Ceramics, Enamels, Glass, Fibre Art, Mixed Media and Collage, Traditional Portraiture, Landscape, Animals, Florals, Still Lifes, Marines (seascapes), etc.

It is possible to work in miniature with any material you have to hand. These discussions are based on the premise that if colour, tone and composition are understood, any materials can be used in any imaginative way you wish.

A *Word about* Size

The Australian Society of Miniature Art has adopted 100 cm^2 (16 in^2) as its maximum size for the painted area (in square format this is 10 cm x 10 cm or 4 in x 4 in, or anything smaller). Any variations could be used, such as 5 cm x 12 cm (2 in x 4¾ in); 2 cm x 2 cm (¾ in x ¾ in); anything, so long as the surface area is no larger than 100 cm^2 (16 in^2). No limit has been set on the frame size by the society. No scale size

has been set, but it is generally understood that to qualify as a miniature work, objects should be miniaturised. A flower painted in actual size would not be considered a miniature.

Frames

Traditional miniatures produced today are often framed in a fine 18-carat-gold plated, oval, locket-style frame, with convex glass to protect the work. These are ideal if the miniature is to hang on the wall of a home, or is to be presented in an exhibition where locked cabinets are provided for display. Such framed miniatures create great security problems for galleries or exhibitions which do not have such provisions.

The move in Australia has been to frame in a larger format, to permit their inclusion in galleries whose policy is to provide wall space if the security risk is kept to a minimum.

The traditional locket frame is not available in Australia at present, but can be obtained from stockists in England.

A less expensive, oval brass frame is usually available. This has been prepared for photographs, and is not the traditional frame, though it often does have convex glass.

It is always important, as with large works on paper, that the glass be kept away from the watercolour. Close contact between glass and artwork creates an environment ideal for the growth of fungus.

If you are framing your work in a larger format, it is important that the framer uses archival (acid-free) mat board between artwork and glass. This acts in the same way as convex glass, in that it leaves a space between the work and the glass.

DIMENSIONS FOR THE FRAMED WORK

No rules for the outer dimensions of the framed work have been set by Australian societies, but individual competitions and exhibitions often do set size restrictions, both in Australia and internationally, so requirements must be read carefully.

For instance, the requirements for the Royal Agricultural Society's Exhibition (Sydney's Royal Easter Show) are at present:

Work can be in any medium, must not exceed 7.5 cm x 7.5 cm [*slightly less than 3 in x 3 in*] on the painted surface, and/or within the mounting or frame, and the maximum dimensions of the framed exhibit must not exceed 15 cm x 15 cm [*just under 6 in x 6 in*].

This exhibition provides a locked cabinet for entries. Slight changes are often made from one year to the next, so it's important to always read the rules to save being rejected on size alone.

Setting up the Studio

As watercolour has generally been accepted as the traditional method for centuries, and many of the suggestions for creative work are based on its use, let's look at the materials you need.

Materials Required:

Artist quality watercolours
No. 3 Kolinsky (Sable) watercolour brush
— and an optional No. 0

1 white palette
2 water containers
1 layout pad of paper
2 pencils — HB and 2B
1 pad or sheet of hot-pressed watercolour paper 300 gsm (140 lbs)
1 old well-washed handkerchief
Magnification
1 kneadable or plastic rubber
1 metal ruler
1 box for storage, and board to act as easel
4 drawing-pins

There are two grades of **watercolour paint**: Student and Artist quality. It is important to purchase the finer quality Artist grade. You will be paying more, but you will have colours with better transparency, and paint which is always able to be reconstituted by the addition of water should it dry out on your palette, so it is never wasted.

For very fine work, the same principle still applies as in the sixteenth century: the brush you use needs to have a very good well, and a very fine tip. A **No. 3 Kolinsky Sable brush** is a very good workhorse. You could add a No. 0 for very fine work if you wish.

Another tip: if you lose the plastic cover which protects the valuable tip of your good brush, a short length of plastic drinking straw will substitute very well. Once the tip is destroyed — and it only takes a minute if you accidentally leave your brush in the water container, tip-end down — the brush will be useless for fine work. If you are not working for some time, place your brushes in a container with some moth balls. Moths love brushes.

Hot-pressed watercolour paper (about 300 gsm/140 lbs) is recommended. Textured and medium-grade watercolour paper (cold-pressed) may be used in some experimental work, but are not suitable for fine work.

An A4 layout pad 210 mm x 197 mm (9 in x 8 in) or any clean scrap paper, can be used for initial rough drawings.

A white palette — a well-sanded plastic lid from an ice-cream container works quite well, but small palettes are now available for miniaturists. They are made of wood, and can be covered with ivorine. These are ideal because you can see at once, when mixing your paint on the palette, the way the colour will look on the painting. (See Suppliers List.)

A small metal ruler is needed to keep the work in miniature size, and to save cutting strips from a wooden ruler when cutting (it happens so easily).

Two water containers are preferable — one to wash the brush and one for dipping.

Two pencils are used — maybe one HB and one 2B, or anything softer. The softer the pencil the more it will smudge, which is great for large work, but frustrating when working small. I find 2B–6B are good 'thinking' pencils, for initial drawings on the layout pad and for doing tonal sketches. HB seems to work best for drawing if there is to be detail.

A kneadable rubber or a firm, white plastic rubber — the kneadable rubber can be worked into a fine point to get into difficult areas, or the firm plastic rubber can be sliced, with a blade, into small wedges, to be used in the same way.

An old, well-washed handkerchief, free of lint, is vital for wiping brushes and cleaning palettes. Tissues are a disaster if used near miniatures. They leave a trail of debris similar to lawn clippings, which are difficult to remove.

Drawing-pins are used to attach work to the easel.

Some form of magnification if you wish. Personally I cannot use a magnifying glass. I find I have this habit of breathing. It occurs often when I hold the glass over my work to place the last details. I prefer a small jeweller's eye glass. You will find what suits you best. I agree with the artists of earlier centuries who warned against using magnification except where necessary. It can sometimes allow design faults to slip through. Just as you need to be able to stand back from a large easel and view your work, you need to be able to see your small work from a distance, from time to time.

A good light focussed on your work should come from left to right if you are right-handed and from right to left if you are left-handed. *Remember:* keep your coffee on your left — washing your brush out in freshly made coffee is bad for the brush.

A box is needed to carry and store all this equipment. If it has a handle, that makes it easier. If the lid, or some other part of it, doubles as an easel, then it is ideal. Originally we made our boxes out of old cedar cigar or chocolate boxes. By covering the lid with green felt and propping it up with a small block of wood, we were able to use the lid as our easel. The box needs to be shallow enough for you to comfortably rest your hand on this easel when working — no more than 4 cm (1½ in) deep.

Today, there is a special miniature box. The palette, with wet paint on it, will slot into an 'air space', so it can be put away or carried easily. Inside there is a removable easel or board, which slots onto the box at a comfortable working angle. This is made of cedar, so that drawing-pins can be easily attached. Everything you require fits inside (see Suppliers List).

The box and easel made for miniaturists showing the working position. Also shown: pencils, brush, old handkerchief, ruler, blade, rubber, magnifying glass, double water container and watercolours. The photo shows the palette ready to paint. Under the palette is the air space in the painting box where a wet palette can be stored and carried, upside down.

You can see that, with all this equipment, you only need a very small space — a corner of the kitchen or bedroom serves quite well. You have to be 'clean in all your doings', as Nicholas Hilliard once said, so the family cannot object — you do not make a mess. All you require is a quiet peaceful corner anywhere — not much to ask.

Supports

HISTORY OF SUPPORTS
In the Middle Ages, parchment and vellum replaced the use of Egyptian papyrus for the preparation of manuscripts. The finer grades of parchment were made from the skin of a newborn animal. Both were made from the skins of calves, goats and sheep. When soaked in water, these skins become wet and pliable. They were stretched, dried and scraped to remove all trace of flesh and hair, and after a lengthy finishing process, provided an excellent support still used by some miniaturists today.

Paper
Initially invented in China in 105 A.D., paper did not come into commercial production in England until the late 1400s. Miniaturists did not use paper as a support until the late 1700s.

Ivory
After the work of Venetian miniaturist, Rosalba Carriera (1675–1757) had been seen, ivory was introduced as a support in England in 1707. Usually a thin, translucent sheet, it was prepared specifically for miniature painters. It is still used today, in many parts of the world, and is generally taken from the tusks of elephants.

Ivorine
Ivorine is also a thin, translucent sheet of material which has been manufactured to replace ivory for the miniaturist. (See also page 41.)

COLOUR OF SUPPORTS
The colour of the traditional support for watercolour has always been white, relying as it does on the white base showing through the transparent wash. This white has been ivory, paper, and, more recently, ivorine. When vellum and parchment were

used, the natural colour of the surface was cream or off-white. Body colour (white) was added to the transparent paint for the initial cover, so that subsequent transparent washes would achieve the glow required.

Ivory has a slight creamy look and, to a lesser extent, so has ivorine. When painted with a transparent wash, both of these surfaces 'glow', particularly when skin is depicted. This is what makes them so suitable for portrait work.

PAPER

Paper comes in different weights. The heavier the paper, the less need there is to stretch it when working in a large format. For miniature work it is not really necessary to stretch the paper, nor is it necessary to have a heavy grade. About 300 gsm (140 lbs) is very pleasant to work on, and rarely buckles unless the work is very wet.

You may like to choose large sheets of different makes of paper, and cut them into small pieces ready for use; or you may prefer to buy small pads already produced by the manufacturer. These are mostly glued around the outer edge, so that it is similar to working on stretched paper.

Just one tip here: if you purchase this type of pad for the first time, you may experience difficulty in removing the sheets as you use them. If you look around the outer glued edge of the pad, you will notice one small area which has not been glued. There is just space enough to slide in a small palette knife or kitchen knife (not serrated). Slide it into the space, on its side and flat with the paper. Gradually work your way around the edge until the sheet is released. If you use a scalpel or serrated knife, you will damage the next sheet of paper and make it difficult to remove later.

Apart from various weights, paper also has three distinct types of surface:

Rough is just that — the surface is rough and great for large work. Highly textured, it has the effect of showing pigment, which drops down in the valley of its surface, sometimes leaving the 'tops' of its hill-like texture white. Unless you are pursuing some particular experimental technique, rough is not really suitable for miniature work.

Hot-pressed paper has been pressed to a smooth satin finish, and is ideal for very small miniature work, where you do not want a surface to intrude.

'Not' means not hot-pressed. It has a medium texture which is very pleasant to use, and works well for slightly larger miniature work where fine detail is not important.

Good quality watercolour paper has a watermark showing the maker's name. This can be seen when the paper is held up to the light. It will always be visible when the full, large sheet is held up to the light. Usually the side where the name can be read correctly is the side the manufacturer has prepared for your work (both sides are not always prepared to receive watercolour).

The watermark is rarely visible on the small prepared pads and, on rare occasions, these pads are prepared upside-down. If you find the paper is receiving the paint a little like blotting paper, then it may be possible you have been unlucky enough to buy a pad where this has happened. All is not lost, but you may have to remove each page and work on the reverse side.

It is important, if you wish your work to last, that you check that the paper you are choosing is acid-free — that it has a neutral pH. Paper which is not marked 'acid-free' is likely to deteriorate and show 'foxing' (brown spots) on the work within a few years. This is very disappointing when you put many hours into painting something special. If you are buying well-known brands such as Arches, Fabriano, Saunders etc., you can be fairly sure that your paper will be neutral, but it is still wise to check the front of your pad or ask your stockist.

Though we have established that the paper is usually white for watercolour, there are various types of white — some which look quite cream. Again, it is a personal choice. If you find you are using watercolour, and leaving a lot of white showing for highlights, you may find these 'whites' are very cold — pure white is a cold colour. You may like to choose a paper which is slightly cream, so that your lights will be warmer.

If you find you cover the whole surface of the paper when you work, then the whiter surface, which will possibly give maximum 'glow' for the transparent wash, may suit you best.

WOOD OR MAT BOARD

Both wood, such as cedar, and mat board, can be used as a support for watercolour. It should be coated first with acrylic gesso (white). This is better if it is applied in many fine coats, and sanded down with fine, wet and dry sandpaper in between coats, to achieve the type of smooth surface required for watercolour. The acrylic gesso forms a moisture-proof coating, so that the watercolour will not sink in when applied.

This is not an easy surface to work on, as it does resist paint; but some very exciting effects can be achieved. It is a good way to start before using ivorine, as it is very similar in the way it reacts. The colour flows on, and other colours can be dropped in. It does not take kindly to having the paint 'pushed around' on its surface and, like ivorine, it is always better to let each coat dry before applying the next.

IVORY

As this old traditional material is no longer easily available (ivory importation to Australia is banned), there seems little value in lengthy discussion, except to comment that if you are lucky enough to track down some old ivory piano keys, you may like to experiment with this support.

These piano keys are often very discoloured, and require cleaning before they can be used. An old toothbrush and toothpaste works very well to bring them to a useable state. They possibly will be yellow with age, and are usually thicker than ivory purchased for painting. It will probably not be possible to trace an image through as you can with ivorine.

IVORINE

'What is it?' is the question everyone asks, and it's difficult to answer, because only the manufacturers really know. I believe one company in England supplies the world demand — and it is in demand throughout the world, as more and more countries are horrified by the senseless destruction of elephants, just for the acquisition of ivory. Ivorine is a substitute for ivory — the support which has been used so consistently since its acceptance in England, in 1720.

About 30 per cent of the accepted entries in the annual exhibition of the Royal Society of Miniature Painters, Sculptors and Gravers, would now be on ivorine, even though ivory is still available in England.

Part Two

CHAPTER 3
Techniques

Pencils

If you are to prepare the finely detailed drawings often required in miniature work, you will require the best pencil and it must be well sharpened.

Pencils, since their development by Conte in France in the early nineteenth century, have been made of a mixture of graphite and clay. The more clay, the harder the pencil and the more graphite content the softer the pencil will be.

The hard range is represented by H to 9H (progressively harder). The soft range is represented by B to 8B (progressively softer). HB is in the middle and seems most useful for the miniaturist. It is soft and grey and does not smudge when preparing fine drawings. The softer B range are excellent for graphite transfers (discussed later) and for exploring tone in initial thumbnail sketches.

The Initial Drawing
Materials Required:
Pencils of your choice — maybe HB and 2B
A layout pad
Kneadable rubber
Ruler
Hot-pressed watercolour paper 300 gsm (140 lbs)
Some simple objects of your choice, arranged as you like.

I have found that a pencil sharpener does not give the length or the fine point required for delicate and detailed drawing. I suggest you use a blade — the type encased in a sturdy metal handle or at least the type of blade which has a shield on one side.

If the pencil is a quality one, the wood will peel back smoothly as you take long sweeping strokes with your blade, down the wood and along the length of the 'lead' (graphite). Rotate the pencil as you sharpen it.

When you have a good length of 'lead' (about 0.8 mm/⅓ in) you are ready to commence. If you keep a piece of fine sandpaper to hand, you can keep the point as sharp as you wish.

Try a hold which may be new for you — four fingers on top of the pencil and thumb underneath. Because the lead you have exposed is very long you will find that you can make large sweeping strokes on a large sheet of paper. Working from the shoulder in this way is a good 'warming up' exercise before you commence the tighter, detailed stroke required for miniature work.

Still life is one of the best places to start. You always have objects around you, no matter where you are. Everything in the kitchen, bedroom or office is grist for the mill. You learn about form, about light hitting objects, about shadows, about reflected light — all this from the simple study of a still life. All this information will be stored away and will help when you turn to portrait, flowers, animal study, landscape or abstract work. No matter what your preference really is, the same rules apply, and, if you choose lighting and inanimate objects which do not change, you can come back day after day. This is not possible with any other form of work. Your sitter may change her hair style, the flowers will die, and even a sloth eventually moves.

Just a few words about the arrangement you choose:

Numbers of objects

Uneven numbers seem to work better than even numbers: three is more satisfying than two; five looks better than four, and so on.

Objects touching

If you arrange three objects in a row, and they are separate from each other — surrounded by space — the painting will have a lonely feel. Fine, if that is the mood you wish to convey. Objects which touch set up a relationship with each other just as people do, and this is conveyed to the viewer. It's not necessary for them all to touch. We don't want to touch everyone we meet — just a special one. So maybe two objects can touch, and one could be set a little apart. This creates a relationship, and a certain tension, which can be exciting.

THE THUMBNAIL SKETCH

When you think about it, no matter how free you wish to work, and how large your work is going to be, you must suffer the restriction of 'edges' or a border. If it were to be a mural on a large wall, you would still need to design within your boundaries, within the given space.

With miniature, as with any work, you have a choice of the shape of that space. It could be:

1. Square
2. Rectangular — Portrait
3. Rectangular — Landscape
4. Oval
5. Circular.

A rectangular space can be viewed in two ways: vertical or horizontal. Vertical is commonly referred to as 'portrait' and horizontal is often referred to as 'landscape', for obvious reasons.

An interesting point about these two divisions of the rectangular shape is that the vertical format is often considered exciting, while the horizontal format is considered restful and relaxing. I think this relates to the fact that while standing we are usually awake, but the body in a prone position could often be found to be asleep.

You will find that you vary in your choice of these two formats, and it may well depend on your mood at the time. But you may like to play with all five choices of shape before making a decision. This is where the thumbnail sketch on a layout block is so helpful. It allows you 'think time' to decide which form you prefer for the subject you have chosen.

Time spent working large and free is time well spent. Time spent looking at the subject and all that surrounds it, and drawing while looking at that subject and *not* at the paper, is even better spent. This puts you in touch with the part of your brain which makes observations and shuts down that other part which says 'I know it all already', and has stopped looking.

That 2B pencil, or an even darker one if you wish, is great for all of this.

Negative space

Negative and positive space. The object (mug) becomes positive space, and the space around it is referred to as negative space.

Another suggestion is to try a continuous line drawing, in large format. Try to follow, with your pencil, the positive space which the object or objects take. Don't worry about the internal structure, just the outer edges, as they form a shape in space. This will give you a division of negative and positive space. Positive space is the subject. Negative space is the space which is not the object. For instance, if the object you are going to draw is a jug, when you draw around its outer edges, you will be making a division of negative and positive space. The hole inside its handle will also be negative space. It often helps to really see the shape of an object by looking at the negative space it takes.

Of course there are times when you just cannot wait to commence. You are so excited by the inspiration to hand that you jump in, and this is great. All these ideas — to work large, try continuous line, to draw, looking at the object — are warming-up exercises, which give you time to play, to loosen up, to get to know your subject and the space around it. They save disappointment later on.

You've done lots of large drawings, and you have decided which format of the five you wish to use. The suggestion is to draw it up roughly on the layout pad. Don't bother ruling at this stage, but remember the dimensions (10 cm x 10 cm [4 in x 4 in], or anything smaller).

SQUINT

Some say to look through your eye lashes. I call that squinting. The object is to reduce your subject to areas of dark and light tone, so that you are no longer concerned with the local colour of the object and its surrounds, but rather with the rhythm and pattern of dark and light. This, in the final painting, is going to make or break your picture. It may be hard to believe.

Stop for a moment and thumb through a book of great paintings of the world. Look through your lashes, or squint at some of them. Notice how the pattern of dark and light through the painting forms a pleasing pattern which satisfies.

This is what you are aiming to produce in your painting, so it is important to see it at this stage.

If you find the arrangement you have set up to draw does not form this pattern, maybe it requires movement of the objects, or that you change your position and draw it from another angle.

Perhaps it would look more pleasing if you were to place it below your eye level, or perhaps above your eye level.

This is the time to make any major

movements. It's too late when you are half-way through your painting, and very distressing.

Now, if you squint again and you see this pattern and find it satisfying, try to express this tone in your first thumbnail sketch. You can do this by using that darker pencil (a 2B or something softer), and just scribbling in the dark areas. Don't worry about any drawing — just the pattern of dark. The white paper will represent the light. Don't worry about the grey areas. It's just dark and light at present — the two ends of the tonal scale.

If you find this placement of tone pleasing and you stay with it, then you can be sure that no matter what colours you use, your painting will work.

I remember being taught that if your tones were correct, you could change all the colours in a painting, and it would still work. It took a long time to come to grips with that statement, but it is true. Look

Darkest tonal areas

Rough tonal drawing on the layout pad. The darks you see when you look through your eyelashes.

again at some of the masters of modern painting. They may paint a green sky, purple trees, and orange foreground — not usually seen in nature, and yet it works.

THE DRAWING
Finally! Would you believe that we could spend so much time in front of these objects, and it's only now that we are ready to draw in miniature? If you have been able to last the distance and restrain yourself, it will be worth it. If you have taken off long before this, and are already painting — great! Rules are meant to be broken in art. They are only there for times of uncertainty.

Draw up the space, this time with a ruler, to the dimensions you have chosen, on hot-pressed watercolour paper. I use the HB pencil here, because it gives me a fine line, but I suggest you keep your drawing light, because HB is not always easy to remove if it digs in deeply.

A little idiosyncrasy of mine is to prepare the entire drawing, and then rub away half of its surface in diagonal strokes. I do have a good reason for this: by this stage I have spent so much time with the objects I know them extremely well. I want to avoid the tightness that comes with painting a completed drawing. So I find that by diagonal erasure, I achieve a 'lost and found' line. This helps to keep the painting 'loose'.

Keep those tonal sketches nearby, because now you are ready to paint.

Backgrounds
The question of how to handle a background becomes problematical, I think, due to a division in our minds between 'subject' and 'background'. Perhaps it comes from our early days at school, in English lessons, when parsing a

sentence into subject and predicate. But when we think about these divisions of a sentence, which were the bane of my life, they are not really divisions: they depend on each other. The dictionary defines *subject* as meaning, 'theme, topic, that about which something is predicated'. It defines *predicate* (and let's substitute background here) as meaning, 'affirm, assert, a statement made about a subject'.

If we were to paint a tree in great detail (our subject) we wouldn't dream of taking the painting inside in search of a red curtain to put behind the tree as its background (though that does launch an idea for a very surreal painting). The area where the tree is growing is an integral part of the tree — it's the predicate: it affirms, asserts and makes a statement about the subject.

The angle of the sun is why you paint the light on the leaves in the way you do; the roots in the ground are why the tree is in that position; the shade on the ground beneath is its shade; the shadows on its trunk have fallen from the trees around it.

I believe that unless your subject exists in a vacuum, it is what it is because of its background — the predicate describes the subject.

I'm spending time on this because it is the question most often asked, and because I think it is so important when first starting to paint. Later, changes can be made, but by then you understand what you are doing.

Colour

Humans have used colour to express themselves and their environment since the first drawings were made on a cave wall. They used the red and yellow earth, the white chalk they had found and made black marks with a burnt fire stick.

Many cultures have contributed since then to expand the range to the rainbow we have today. The Egyptians added Malachite (green) and Azurite (blue bice) and Madder (a blue-red). The Greeks added white lead and an artificially produced red-vermilion. This red was in common use by the fifteenth century. Adopted by the illuminators, it was called 'minium' and it is thought, by some, that the word 'miniature' may have come from the use of minium by the limners.

New colours have been added and subtracted through the centuries but there are still three primary colours which form the basic structure on which all colour is built.

Colour requirements

6 x 5 mL (17 fl oz) tubes of Artist quality watercolour in the following colours:

1. Winsor Yellow
2. Indian Yellow
3. Cadmium Red
4. Alizarin Crimson
5. Ultramarine Blue
6. Cobalt Blue

A tube of white gouache can be added for later exercises (I use Pelikan brand).

Colour Theory

Let's look at colour. There will be many artists who have been painting for a long time, and have their own collection of colours, perhaps carefully chosen to suit individual preferences, or perhaps accumulated on a whim.

The suggestions offered here are really for those who are purchasing artist quality for the first time and would like to consider the options, or for those who have trouble mixing colour, and unintentionally make 'mud'.

Cezanne once said that if you showed

him mud, he would show you a rainbow; and when you think of the beautiful colours of autumn: russet, caramel and olive, you understand what he meant.

Initially, we cannot control brown: we hit it accidentally, and we are disappointed and frustrated. Yet brown is just the equal mix of the three primary colours: red, blue and yellow.

PRIMARY COLOURS

We can make all the colours of the rainbow with the three primary colours, but we cannot mix the primary colours from other colours. So, if we have red, blue and yellow, that's all we need — but which red, blue and yellow? When you go to purchase, you will be faced with many decisions. With red alone, you will be offered a choice of 19 colours which could all be called 'red'. With blue, the choice is less — about 11. With yellow, you would need to choose from 15. So how do you choose?

If you look carefully at a colour chart, you will notice that there are differences between the reds, the blues and the yellows. This difference, if it is analysed, is really due to the amount of red or blue in each colour. Red tends to warm a colour, and blue tends to make it cold.

THE DOUBLE PRIMARY SYSTEM

If yellow has a percentage of blue in it, it tends to be colder. If yellow has a percentage of red in it, it tends to be warmer. This is where yellow sits in the rainbow (or spectrum) — between red and blue; so it can be influenced by both. It is possible to choose from the chart both a cold yellow and a warm yellow. Blue is positioned between red and yellow. As blue moves closer to red, it is warmed by it; as it moves away towards yellow, it becomes

cooler. It's possible to choose a warm blue, and a cold blue.

Red sits between blue and yellow. As it moves closer to blue, it becomes colder. Again, we can choose a warm red and a cold red.

This gives us a double primary system — two of each colour: two yellows, two blues and two reds. Now you can really start to work with colour, because from these you can mix every colour including black, and all those beautiful 'mud' colours of russet, caramel and olive.

It takes time for your eye to see these subtle differences in the primary colours, so I am suggesting six colours. As you become accustomed to them, I'm sure you will choose your own.

The colours chosen to represent the cold primaries are: Winsor Yellow, Alizarin Crimson (red) and Cobalt Blue.

The colours to represent the warm primaries are: Indian Yellow, Cadmium Red and Ultramarine Blue.

The choice of these particular colours was based on an 'A' or 'AA' rating for permanence, and the lowest possible 'S' rating ('S' indicates price, based on the degree of difficulty in obtaining the pigment).

The triangle (next page) shows three primaries — Winsor Yellow, Cobalt Blue and Cadmium Red (two cold and one warm). They form a base to build your own colour wheel, if you wish.

BUILDING YOUR OWN COLOUR STAR

1. Start by inscribing a circle. A radius of 3 cm (1¼ in) has been used here.
2. Mark off three points on the circumference with the same distance as the radius. These will form the three points of a triangle.
3. Form an inverted triangle by the same

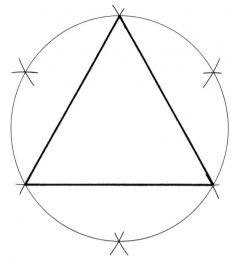

The basic triangle, formed by inscribing the radius on the circumference of the circle.

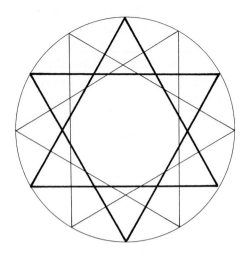

Adding two more triangles gives a twelve-pointed star.

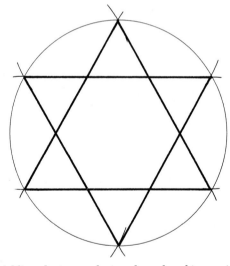

Adding the inverted triangle and making a six-pointed star.

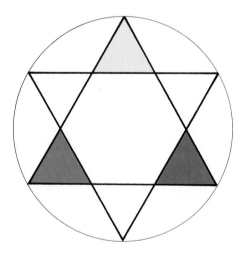

The first triangle painted with three primary colours: Winsor Yellow — Cadmium Red — Cobalt Blue.

method. You now have a six-pointed star.

First Set of Primary Colours If you paint Winsor Yellow at the top, Cadmium Red to the left, and Cobalt Blue to the right of the first triangle, you will have a base of three primaries.

Secondary Colours The secondary colours are made by the mixture of two primaries. Blue and yellow together make green; red and blue form purple; and yellow and red form orange. The three primaries have made three new colours: green, purple and orange. If you are going to paint these into the corners of that

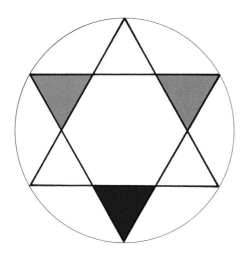

*The inverted triangle painted with the
secondary colours:*
Orange (Winsor Yellow + Cadmium Red);
Green (Winsor Yellow + Cobalt Blue);
Purple (Alizarin Crimson + Ultramarine Blue).

inverted triangle, use Winsor Yellow and
Cobalt Blue to make a rather sweet green;
Cadmium Red and a bigger percentage of
Winsor Yellow for orange; but you will
need Alizarin Crimson and Ultramarine to
make the best purple. If you look at the
larger twelve-pointed star, you will see why
this is so. Alizarin Crimson and
Ultramarine are near each other in the
spectrum and, as they naturally merge with
each other, they form purple.

Complementary Colours If you look
at the six-pointed star, you will see that
Winsor Yellow is directly opposite purple.
They complement each other, and are
called 'complementary colours'. Orange is
directly opposite blue, and is its
complement. Red is opposite green and, so
again, is its complement.

This innocent little piece of information
is possibly the most important part of the
colour theory, and often proves to be the
most difficult part to absorb. Its knowledge
will help you darken or 'tonally dull'
colours instantly. When a small percentage
of one is used against a mass of the other,
the colours 'glow'. You can imagine a spot
of orange glowing on a sea of blue!

The system works in forward and
reverse. A *small* percentage of yellow added
to purple will dull the purple. A *small*
percentage of purple added to yellow will
dull the yellow. Each colour added to its
complement works in the same way.

The reason I stress *small percentage* is as
follows. If you analyse it, with purple
added to yellow, what you are really doing
is adding a mixture of red and blue to
yellow. If you mix these three primary
colours in equal amounts, as mentioned
before, you will just get brown or 'mud'.

**Remembering Complementary
Colours** This is so important I am
suggesting another way to remember
complementary colours with constant
reference to a colour wheel. Let's go back
to the simplicity of the three primary
colours. Imagine you have three pieces of
cellophane, red, blue and yellow (better
still, if you can actually have them in front
of you, try this). If you move the red over
blue, you will make purple. The colour left
out is yellow. That is the complementary
colour. If you place the red over yellow,
you will make orange. The colour which
remains is blue. That is its complementary
colour. If you place yellow over blue, you
make green. The colour left is red, its
complementary colour.

Making Black If you mix the three
primary colours with extra blue, you will
make black. The best black, with the
colours we are using, is made by mixing a
strong purple, using Alizarin Crimson and
Ultramarine Blue (a very blue purple), and
the addition of a small percentage of

Winsor Yellow. It's logical isn't it? Complementary colours darken.

Making Russet, Caramel and Olive by Choice (Beautiful 'mud'.) Mixing different combinations of the secondary colours, orange, green and purple, will give you the control you require over 'mud'. Orange and purple will give you russet.

It could be shown this way:

Orange (red + yellow) + purple (red + blue) = russet

The percentage of red is greater in this mix.

Purple (blue + red) + green (blue + yellow) = olive

The percentage of blue is greater.

Green (yellow + blue) + orange (red + yellow) = caramel

The percentage of yellow is greater. So we have achieved what Cezanne promised.

Adding White Now, if you wish to add a tube of white, you can make the most beautiful 'tints' imaginable — all from your original six tubes of colour. Watercolourists depend on the white of the paper to make these subtle colours. When you add tube white, you are actually making your own 'gouache'.

The Second Set of Primary Colours It's time to look at that second set of primary colours, and see where they sit. We have used Winsor Yellow (cold), Cadmium Red (warm), and Cobalt Blue (cold) to make the first triangle; and discovered that you need to use Alizarin Crimson and Ultramarine Blue to make the deepest purple, because these colours are close together. If you look at the twelve-pointed star, you will see that Alizarin Crimson and Ultramarine Blue fall either side of purple, and that the warm Indian Yellow is next to Winsor Yellow, but closer

The twelve-pointed star, showing the position of the double primary colours, secondary colours and additional mixes of orange and green. Inner additions show each colour mixed with white (tints). Arrows on the outside of the star show the direction when using dissonance.

to red, and this explains its warmth.

You can see that the other colours in the twelve-pointed star, which have not yet been discussed, are formed on the left by degrees of the mixture of Cadmium Red and yellow, and on the right by degrees of the mixture of yellow and Cobalt Blue. Inside the star, you will see each of these colours mixed with white.

They say that theories are only useful when you strike trouble. In moments of strength, problems are solved intuitively, and that is as it should be. I am suggesting this colour theory only for those who have struck trouble. Each artist has a favourite palette, this is only one such palette.

Yet there are reasons for ploughing through all this theory. If you wish to achieve distance or depth in your painting, whether it be still life, portrait, landscape, traditional or modern, a knowledge of colour will solve most of your problems.

If you are taught to use a certain set of colours for one painting, and you do not understand why, then you will be unable to work on your own. I believe very strongly in the theory:

Feed a man fish and you feed him for a day — Teach a man to fish and you feed him for life.

The reason so much time is spent on colour theory, tone and composition is that once grasped, you can flow from one medium to another without special tuition — you understand the basics.

ACHIEVING DEPTH IN PAINTING

1. Objects in the distance are smaller.
2. Colours in the distance are tonally closer together.
3. Objects in the distance are less sharp — more fuzzy in appearance.
4. The darkest darks, and the lightest lights, need to be closest to you.
5. Warm colours advance; cool colours recede.
6. Break all the above rules if something exciting is happening in your painting, and you are flying high on intuition.

DISSONANCE

Here is a little addition to colour theory which you may totally ignore, and still live happily ever after — but, if you would like to take the time to come to grips with its meaning, it will make small gems glow.

The dictionary defines dissonance as 'a mingling of discordant sounds', but it is synonymous with 'inconsistent' and 'contradictory', and herein lies the clue to its use in painting. It can be used when you are trying to express light falling on an object. Normally, watercolourists leave white paper to express light. Oil painters, pastellists, gouache and acrylic artists may express light. Oil painters, pastellists, gouache and acrylic artists may express light on an object by choosing a lighter colour than the surrounding colours and mixing it with white; for example, yellow mixed with white to make a light lemon colour, used as a highlight on orange.

With dissonance you use a theory which is quite 'inconsistent' and 'contradictory'. If your subject is an orange (the fruit), and you wish to show the light, you go backwards on the colour star to a warm red, mix it with white so that it becomes pink, and add this to the area of light on the orange. Can you imagine how beautiful this can look? But it is a contradiction. It is opposite to everything we have been taught — but it works.

The same effect can be achieved in watercolour by first washing over the fruit with a very weak and pale red (pink), and then painting all but one spot with orange, the 'local colour' (real colour), leaving the first wash of pink exposed where the light is reflected.

Looking at the colour star, choosing colours to achieve dissonance works in an anticlockwise direction to the left-hand side of the star, and in a clockwise direction on the right-hand side. Going in an anticlockwise direction:

A lemon could have a pale orange highlight.
An orange could have a pale pink highlight.
A red apple could have a pale mauve highlight.
A purple plum could have a blue-red (Alizarin) highlight.

Going in a clockwise direction:

A lemon could have a pale green highlight.
A green pear could have a pale blue highlight.
A dark blue grape could have a mauve highlight.
A purple plum could have a warm blue (Ultramarine) highlight.

You will notice that in the case of the lemon at the top of the star, and the plum at the bottom of the star, you have a choice — to move clockwise or anticlockwise — in the colour you choose.

That's dissonance — a contradiction, but it can be used in many situations, not only with fruit. It can be used in portrait, clothing, landscape … anywhere as long as it is not overused. Just as in music, a discordant note can add a touch of surprise and excitement; too many such notes create disharmony.

Understanding Tone

Black, grey and white — everyone understands tone in this language. Black is the darkest tone we know; white is the lightest; and all the greys come in between, and can be called mid-tones.

We are accustomed to photographs where images are reproduced in black and white (and all the greys in between). If you think about it, you realise the people in the picture were not having a 'grey day' when they were photographed, nor were they necessarily wearing black and white. They were photographed in full living colour, but what we are seeing is each colour in the image being presented by a tonal range through black, grey and white. The connection we need to make in our minds if we are to come to grips with tone is how black, white and grey relate to colour.

If you were to take that same black,

white and grey photograph, and try to paint it in the colours you imagine the person may have been wearing, you may not be able to pick the colour, but you would be able to pick the strength of that colour — its tone.

Let's say the subject of the photograph is a man in a dark suit — not black but very dark grey; you know instinctively that the suit could not have been yellow — yellow is a very light colour; but it could have been navy blue, or dark green or dark brown — these are all low-key colours which could be represented by a dark grey in a photograph.

In miniature painting, an understanding of tone is important if your painting is to 'carry', or sustain interest. It entices the viewer to look closer to see the gem you have so carefully painted.

If you squint at the surroundings you are in now, you will notice that a lot of colour fades away, and objects take on a black, grey and white look. If you were to take a soft black pencil and trace just the blacks, you would notice that they form a pattern, and often show the shapes of objects. In fact if you do this carefully, you will be amazed at how much of your surroundings you will depict — with just the 'darks' showing on a sheet of white paper.

Have you ever seen a photograph which has been run through a photostat machine? Sometimes it appears as just black and white. You can still tell a lot about the image, but there are no greys — they have dropped out. This is sometimes referred to as a 'tone drop'. Although the grey tones have been dropped, you can still read the picture — even from a distance. The black tones follow a pattern which flows through the image and we can recognise it.

A 'tone drop' showing mainly black and white, with little or no grey; and yet the painting can still be 'read'.

Patricia Moy. 'One morning at Ken's'. Watercolour on paper. Image size 6 cm x 6 cm (2⅜ in x 2⅜ in). In a private collection.

If a miniature contains the same ingredients — a pattern of dark colour which flows through and allows a viewer to 'read it', even from a distance — then it is likely to intrigue the onlooker.

Miniatures in general exhibitions have enormous competition, being hung, as they often are, cheek by jowl with large work. For them to be effective at all, they need to have this ability to intrigue — to coax a closer look.

If you look at the colour reproduction of the painting 'One morning at Ken's', and then at the black, white and grey reproduction of the same painting, you will see where the different tones sit on the scale. The red of the geraniums is a surprisingly low-key colour. It reproduces as black.

The orange flowers on the cushion reproduce as a mid-tone grey, as does the

A black, grey and white image of the same painting. The reds are surprisingly low-key, and appear as black, while the blue-grey light on the tablecloth is a high-key colour, and registers as white.

pale grey shadow on the cloth, and the pink geranium in the pot. Mid-key paintings usually contain pink, light green, light blue, orange and mauve.

The lighter pale blue-grey area of light on the tablecloth reproduces as white. This is the high-key area of the painting. If you squint at the colour reproduction, you will see it in the same range of black, through grey to white.

High-key colours are all those closest to white: yellow, very pale pink, pale blue, pale green. It's easy to remember if you think of feeling high, light-headed and bright. Paintings in these colours are said to be high-key paintings.

Dark colours like purple, dark green, many reds, and deep blue are usually found in quantity in low-key paintings. An easy way to remember is to think of feeling low, heavy and in a dark mood.

If you look at your own paintings, you may find that you generally fit into one of these areas; that you are naturally comfortable using high-key colours, but rarely experiment with low-key colours. Or you may find that you stay in the middle range, using bright strong colours. It helps to see where your painting range lies, and it is fun to explore other areas and extend your range.

A quick, easy way to play with tone, and to help understand it, is to use collage. Here is a suggestion:

1. Armed with old glossy magazines, scissors and glue, cut out as many colours as you can which you see as low-key colours (darks).
2. Cut them into small pieces and paste them onto a small drawn area about 10 cm x 10 cm (4 in x 4 in).
3. Squint at the square when you have finished. If any of the pieces 'jump' (don't blend in with the others), it will be because they are not in the same tonal range, and do not belong.

This is a much quicker way to learn about tone.

You may like to try the same exercise with mid-tones, and then with light tones. If you keep these samples, you will always have a reference when you are looking to mix tones which are the same. Finding tones which are the same in different colours is a difficult exercise, but is well worth the time spent no matter which way you intend to work, traditional or contemporary.

Part Three

Moy

CHAPTER 4
Watercolour on Paper

Nicholas Hilliard in his essay (*c.* 1600) 'Treatise concerning the Arte of Limning' (Thornton, R. K. J. and Cain, T. G. S., *Nicholas Hilliard's The Arte of Limning*, 1981) had much to say about the atmosphere required by the miniaturist:

The first and chiefest precepts which I give you is cleanliness, and therefore fittest for a gentleman, that the practise of limning be pure and clearly in all his doings ... beware you touch not your work with your fingers ... neither breathe on it, especially in cold weather. Take heed of the dandruff of the head shedding from the hair and of speaking over your work for sparkling, for the least sparkling of spittal will never be helpful if it light on the face or any part of the naked. Discreet talk or reading, quiet mirth or music offendeth not but shorteneth the time and quickeneth the spirit, both in the drawer and he which is drawn; also in anywise avoid anger, shut out questioners and busy fingers.

This is excellent advice, and is still applicable today.

Materials Required:
Artist quality watercolours
No. 3 and No. 0 Kolinsky Sable brushes
1 white palette
Hot-pressed watercolour paper
300 gsm (140 lbs)
Water containers

Setting out the palette is a good place to start with watercolour. If you have never used watercolour before there is hope, because the way you start will be the way you will continue, and you won't get into bad habits as some of us have done.

If you set the colours out the way they are placed in the colour star, and always do it the same way, then in time, you will not even have to look. You will know instinctively where to reach for the colour you want. If you are using the colours suggested, then you can start anywhere you like on the star. I like to keep them across the top of the palette, so there is room to mix colours.

If you squeeze out Cobalt Blue first in the top left-hand side of the palette then

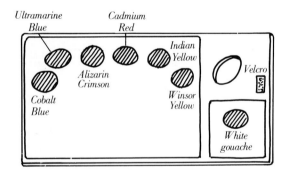

Two pieces of ivorine have been glued to the wooden palette — one large and one small. The large piece has six colours and the small piece holds white separate from the colours. In this way white will not intermix with the colours. A small piece of velcro holds the palette (upside-down) when carried in the painting case.

the colours would follow this order:

Cobalt Blue — Ultramarine Blue —
Alizarin Crimson — Cadmium Red —
Indian Yellow — Winsor Yellow

Because watercolour is such a gentle
medium, or can be, and because we are
talking about miniatures, many feel that
you just need a very small amount of paint
squeezed out, but you will find that this
will restrict you. My suggestion is that you
squeeze out plenty of colour. Maybe as
much of each colour as the size of your
thumbnail.

Because, hopefully, you are using artist's
colours, you will easily be able to re-wet
your colours whenever you want to, so
there is no wastage.

Take time off to play with the colour, so
that you come to understand the amount
you will need on your brush, the amount
of water you will need to add, and how it
acts on your paper.

Hot-pressed paper is best for miniatures,
because it is satin smooth. You can use a
rough- or medium-textured cold-pressed
paper if you wish, but it will spoil any fine
detail you may want to paint. Your colours
will respond in different ways, depending
on the paper you choose. It's worth buying
a small pad of each of a good acid-free
brand, so that you can try for yourself.

To commence, wet your brush and take
a small amount from the freshly squeezed
paint. Place this on the area of clear palette
underneath. Take a brush-full of water, and
gently mix this with the paint on the
palette until water and paint are
thoroughly mixed. Paint this mix across
your sheet of paper, and look at it carefully.
If you can see spots of pigment or if it
looks 'streaky', it requires more mixing.
Don't be tempted to push the colour

around with your brush once you have put
it down. This often spoils watercolour. The
appeal lies in its freshness. The paper, once
wet, is in a tender state, and brushing it
merely agitates the fragile surface, and
muddies the look of the work.

When the patch you have painted is
thoroughly dry place another stroke of the
same colour alongside it. You will notice a
vast difference in colour. This is worth
remembering: watercolour always dries
much lighter — something to keep in mind
with your original mix. You can always
make it stronger than you think you will
require.

Next you could try wetting an area of
paper, and then dropping on your mixed
colour. See how the colour only spreads
where the water is? This is worth
remembering too. It means that you can
wet any area of your painting first, and
when you drop colour in, the paint will
stay in the area you have wet and not
stray. When this area dries and you
compare it with the first stroke you
painted, you will see that it is even lighter
than the first. The extra water has diluted
the strength of the colour even more —
another reason to keep that original mix
pretty strong.

Mixing Colours

How about a combination of two colours?
If you mix Cobalt Blue and Winsor Yellow
together equally, you will achieve a rather
'sweet' green. You could paint this green
on the paper, and then try it another way.
This time mix the Cobalt Blue well with
water, and at the last minute add Winsor
Yellow to your brush and paint with it. See
what exciting things happen? Your eye
allows the colours to combine, and it is
more interesting than the straight mix of
colours. This is what watercolour is about.

Mixing a Touch of a Complementary Colour

Remember, as stated earlier, if you mix a combination of Cobalt Blue and Winsor Yellow, and you find the green too 'sweet', you can use your knowledge of the complementary colour system and darken it with just a touch of red (its complement). Too much and your mix will turn brown, because you will have three primaries mixed in equal proportions. It just needs a touch.

Wet-In-Wet and Hard-Edge Painting

You hear a lot about 'wet-in-wet' watercolour. It is another exciting aspect of the medium.

Wet an area of paper again, and drop that same Cobalt Blue and Winsor Yellow mix on to the wet area. Try to quickly add a drop of Ultramarine Blue to one corner; as it spreads, quickly add a smaller drop of Alizarin Crimson to the same corner, and watch what happens. This is a wet-in-wet technique. You will probably see that there is some noticeable 'granulation' of the pigment. The heavier particles have separated from the lighter ones. This effect is something the watercolourist often tries to achieve with a knowledge of certain mixes of colours, and their tendency to separate.

CAULIFLOWERS OR SPIDERS

When you are working this way with wet-in-wet, you have to move very quickly. All the paints on your palette need to be very wet and ready to pick up on the brush. If, for some reason, you delay when you are going to drop on the second or the third colour, you may notice strange little curly marks in the painted area as it dries. This

seems to occur when the first colour put down was already starting to dry before the second colour was dropped. Some artists like the effect of these marks, which are called 'cauliflowers' or 'spiders'. If you like them, you know how to make them.

DROPPING COLOUR

Just a word about dropping colour: it really works best to do just that. It's quite a different technique from the one we learnt at school, where you loaded the brush and drew it towards you, across the page, holding the bristles rather flat to the page. When dropping a colour, you are holding a brush loaded with colour just on top of an area of paper which is wet, and allowing the wetness of the paper to take the load from the brush. The brush itself does not really touch the paper: it touches only the 'wetness'.

Adding Colour to Dry Paint

When you are adding fresh watercolour to paint which is dry, it is a good idea to wet (with water) a larger area than you require. Add the paint where you want it to be. By doing this, you will have soft edges where the fresh paint has been added, rather than hard edges, which happen when wet paint is added to a dry surface.

It's worth using this method when you are 'glazing' (strengthening a colour or going over a colour with the complementary colour). Once again it avoids forming hard edges.

Adding White

Most watercolours are regarded as transparent, and when white is added they are said to become opaque. Opaque white is often referred to as 'body colour'. The early miniaturists called the opaque colour they mixed the 'carnation'.

Gouache, which can be purchased in tubes, is also watercolour with body colour added. Although I may refer to the use of gouache from time to time in this book, I mean gouache which is made by adding artist's quality watercolour to opaque white. There is a difference. The quality of the artist's watercolour is more permanent, and you are able to control the level of transparency when you mix your own body colour.

Chinese white, used by many watercolourists to add white to a painted area when required, has not been found to mix well when a body colour is required. Pelikan White has been found to be more versatile.

Even though watercolours are regarded as transparent, some are more transparent than others.

Transparent and Opaque Colours

It is a great help to understand which are the transparent and which are the opaque colours when you are using watercolours, and it's easy to find out.

Take some Indian ink and an old brush, and sweep a line of black across an old sheet of watercolour paper. Wait for it to dry. Now take the colours we are using, and paint a strong brush-stroke of paint with each colour across the line, at right angles to it. Allow these to dry. It's important to paint with equal strength with each colour.

Now, if you look at the area where the colour crosses the ink line, you should see two reactions. Some of the colours will be visible on top of the ink line — these will be the opaque colours. Some will seem to have disappeared as they cross the line — these will be the transparent colours.

Usually, Alizarin Crimson, Ultramarine Blue and Indian Yellow seem to be more transparent, whilst Cadmium Red, Cobalt Blue and Winsor Yellow will appear more opaque.

This information is useful to have when you want to use colours to 'glaze'. Glazing is used when you want to intensify a colour, or when you want to darken it tonally. For instance, if you had used orange as a colour in the background, and you found it was too 'warm' and you wanted to 'send it back' (make it less intrusive), you could wash it over with a glaze of thin blue (its complement). Even though Ultramarine is a warmer blue, it would still be my choice, because it is more transparent and less likely to become muddy when used as a glaze.

If you want to avoid any chance of stirring up an under-colour when glazing, there is something you can do which may surprise you if you have not used watercolour before. You can take a brush of clean water, and wash over the area where the dry under-colour is. Allow this water wash to dry, and then go ahead and glaze. This sets the first colour, and stops it mixing with the second layer, or glaze. This would only work when using watercolour on paper. It would not be possible to work this way on ivorine. If glazing on ivorine, you would wash straight over with the glazing colour, maybe trying William Wood's technique of 'breathing' on the under-layer first — just to soften it a little.

CHAPTER 5
Dry-Brush Watercolour

This is a technique which was developed to work on materials like vellum, which swells and buckles when too much water is added. The term is misleading: the paint is dry; but the brush is really damp.

There are different styles of working in dry-brush. Andrew Wyeth, an American artist who works with watercolour and tempera, uses a dry-brush style. He fans the tip of his brush out with his fingers, so that many strokes are made at the same time.

For miniature work, the style is slightly different: tiny strokes are applied one at a time, and very close to each other. Each stroke may be as small as 0.5 mm (⅛ in). They must not touch, or the purpose of the stroke will be lost as they blend together.

The entire painting is worked from the lightest tone through to the darkest tone, waiting in between each layer for the under-layer to dry before applying the next. Some of each layer is left to express the tone in the area.

Colours are mixed and allowed to dry in small puddles on the palette. The strength of the tone can be built up by the application of the same colour stroked on top or by the addition of a second colour.

It may help to practise the small stroke with a well-sharpened HB pencil. Mark out an area 1 cm x 1 cm (½ in x ½ in), and see how many tiny strokes you can fit in to this area. It's quite possible to make 250

In this small area of 1 square centimetre (³⁄₈ in²), there are over 250 pencil strokes. It's not a bad way to practise the stroke required for dry-brush.

strokes or more, so you can see how small the marks need to be. If you work with magnification, you would make many more strokes to the square centimetre (square inch).

Working in Dry-Brush in an Area 23 mm (1 in) in Diameter

Materials Required:
Hot-pressed watercolour paper
No. 3 Kolinsky Sable brush
Watercolours
Water containers
Old handkerchief.

This technique is ideal when you are working in a very small area, and wish to express a lot of detail.

The size is taken from an Australian ten cent coin, and the challenge is to design a landscape in the round — a subject more usually painted in a horizontal or vertical format. Once your thinking gets in the 'mode' of small and round, it's not really difficult.

With the topic chosen, the search is on for the lightest tone. This will be the area of greatest light. You can put on larger areas of light wash first, if you wish, before starting to use dry-brush, or complete the whole painting in the dry-brush style.

TO COMMENCE

Mix up some of the lightest colours you are going to use. Mix them in thin puddles, which will dry quickly — about the size of the top of your thumb for a work as small in area as this.

While the colour is drying, you may like to make yourself comfortable for a long haul ahead. Ensure your drawing has been sketched in lightly, that it has been attached to a sheet of clean paper, and is pinned to your easel; that the light is good and focussed on your work; and how about a cup of something hot, and some quiet music in the background?

PAINTING TECHNIQUES

Now the paint will be dry. With your hot drink placed well to the left (if you are right-handed), and that old linen handkerchief in your left hand, dip your brush in clean water, wash it out well, then gently pass it through the handkerchief in a wiping action from just above the ferrule to the tip.

There are two reasons for this. The first is to stop the dreaded drip, which always sits on the ferrule, waiting to drop its load when you least expect it, and where you least want it. The second is because the brush needs to be slightly damp, but not wet, when making this delicate stroke.

Roll the tip of the brush in the dry puddle of paint. This rolling action helps to keep the tip well pointed. You will probably be surprised how much of the puddle you can pick up with the damp

brush. You will be able to work many strokes with this one dip. Now you can understand why a single hair brush would be of little value. You would have to move back to the puddle for every stroke with such a brush.

You may choose to make tiny strokes, side by side; or tiny dots; or you may prefer to cross-hatch, coming back over your first strokes at an angle. You will find the way you like best. If you do choose stipple (tiny dots) you may be better to use a short, stubby, but finely pointed brush made specially for stipple. Constant stipple strokes are not good for a brush with any length of hair, as they tend to spoil the tip.

STARTING FROM THE LIGHTEST TONE

When you find the area of lightest tone — perhaps it's a spot where the sun shines on a patch of grass — work over the whole area of grass with that lightest tone. When the area is dry, come back with the same colour on your brush, and go over with the

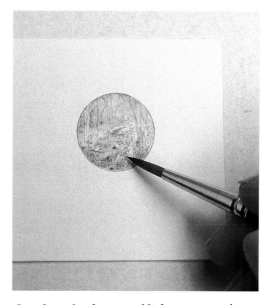

Searching for the area of lightest tone, and placing it in first.

same tiny strokes, leaving the area of greatest light. Continue this way, gradually deepening the colour very slowly.

IMPRESSIONIST'S STYLE

You may like to try some visual colour mixing as the impressionists did. Place colours side by side, instead of mixing them, allowing the viewer's eye to make the mix. Instead of mixing orange, you could place strokes of yellow and red next to each other, allowing the eye to make orange. Blue and yellow placed next to each other will allow the eye to see green, and so on.

Gradually work over the whole area of your painting, deepening tone as you go, always allowing the under-colour to dry first.

Finished work painted in the dry-brush method: 'Forest Spirits Number 2'. Patricia Moy. Image size 2.5 cm diameter (1 in).

CHAPTER 6
Watercolour on Ivorine

Ivorine is the substance which fascinates everyone new to miniature work. It is a thin, translucent sheet of a plastic-like material which has become a substitute for ivory in many countries.

It is thought that, originally, the thin sheets were coated with powdered ivory from tusks. This was to provide artists with a new support as ivory became increasingly expensive. Ivorine is said to contain no ivory today as a vegetable product is now used as a coating.

Ivorine is sold in England and is now available from a limited number of stockists in Australia (see Suppliers List). It comes in single sheets or in packs of 25 and can be purchased in large or small sheets. I tend to use the small sheet which is 14.5 cm x 20 cm (about 6 in x 8 in).

Materials Required:
1 sheet of ivorine 14.5 cm x 20 cm
(6 in x 8 in)
1 sharp blade and scissors
1 layout pad
2 pencils (HB and 2B)
2 brushes No. 3 and No. 0 Kolinsky Sable
All Artist Watercolours
2 water containers
3 drawing-pins
Removable adhesive.

Ivorine warps easily with changes in temperature so keep it under pressure until you are ready to use it.

Grease is the biggest enemy (from fingermarks) so try to handle it without touching the surface. Its surface will take: pencil, watercolour, oil, gold leaf, and acrylic. In fact, anything you wish to use but, because of its translucency, it is best used when some of its porcelain-like quality is allowed to show through. Gouache (watercolour with white) is a little heavy on its surface and defeats the purpose of its use.

I'm discussing watercolour on ivorine here but once you have prepared the surface carefully you may use any medium you prefer.

Ivorine has an advantage over paper. Mistakes can be completely washed off. It will not break down in time as will some paper. It may yellow slightly with age and exposure to light.

Because of its off-white colour and translucency, it works just as ivory does, to represent light on skin, so it has proved to be an excellent substitute for ivory. Drawings can be placed underneath and can be seen well enough to trace through the image. This is another advantage over paper.

Working on Ivorine
1. Cut sheets larger than required.
2. Clean the surface thoroughly.
3. Sand down the surface with fine sandpaper, then wash it over with water.

4. Trace an image if necessary, with colour on a fine brush.

5. Remove the original drawing, and set the ivorine on a clean sheet of paper. Place the drawing alongside for reference.

6. Commence painting, allowing each layer to dry before applying the next.

If you follow all these steps, you should be happy with your results. Ivorine is not an easy surface to work on, at first. It is a little like painting on the plastic lid of an ice-cream container. Some dislike it, and do not persist, but there are quite a few advantages in learning to use it. The enemy is always dirt and grease. One fingermark on ivorine, and the paint just will not take.

It may be a good idea to practise on a scrap, and just play at first. Load a brush with colour, and wash it over the surface. You will soon see how it will resist any greasy areas, and how noticeable any small hairs or pieces of lint are on its surface.

You have probably made a decision about the size you wish to work within, and have prepared your drawing on paper.

The next step is to cut a piece of ivorine, preferably with a blade against a metal ruler, and resting on a firm piece of cardboard or on a cutting mat. You have to press down quite firmly, and sometimes repeat the cut. I tend to cut a little larger than my image size for two reasons: it allows me to hold the work without putting my fingers on the area where I wish to paint; and it leaves a surround for the framer to cover with the mat board, so that he will not have to encroach on the painted surface. If I am going to work in an oval or round format, I would mark out the image area, but I would still cut the piece of ivorine in a rectangular or square shape, for the same reasons.

Now is the time to wash the cut piece well with detergent. Dry it very carefully with that old linen handkerchief. It is a good idea at this stage to go over the surface with the finest sandpaper you can find. I tend to sand once vertically, and once horizontally, so that any marks left will give a 'linen finish'. Dust off with a fine brush. Now, run a brush loaded with water only, over the surface, and check the surface agaist the light, to make sure there are no resist areas.

Tracing on to Ivorine

A light box, if you have one, is very handy here. It is much easier to trace the work when it is lit from beneath. A sheet of perspex or glass, raised on two bricks, or heavy books, with a small table light placed on its side, so that it shines up and through the glass sheet, works quite well. The other alternative is to use what has been called 'the poor-man's light box': a well-lit window. In this case, tape your drawing to the window, and then tape the ivorine on top of the drawing. You will be able to see through quite clearly.

If all this fails, you can always transfer the drawing by shading over the back of the image with a soft pencil (2B–6B), so that you make a type of carbon, or in this case graphite, transfer. You then place the drawing face-up over the ivorine, and redraw it with an HB pencil. The rubbed graphite on the back will transfer the drawing to the ivorine. Personally, I would use this method on paper, but I would prefer not to use it on ivorine, as I think it tends to dirty the surface a little.

Ready to Paint

With a piece of removable gum, attach the ivorine over your prepared drawing (if you are going to trace through), or over a clean sheet of paper, and attach the drawing or paper with drawing-pins to your easel in a comfortable position. Unless you have a reason to want your paint to run, you are really better to have your easel flat when working on ivorine, so that the paint will stay where you put it.

You can start by putting on large washes, if you wish, but you will need to work in areas removed from each other, unless you want them to run together. You can put one colour on, and drop another colour into it, if you like; or wait until each wash is dry before gently applying the next. You can try stipple strokes, or dry brush-strokes over a dried wash. You can put a wash over an area, and then lift-off back to white with a damp brush, and apply another colour where you have lifted-off, or leave the area the colour of the ivorine. It is much easier to work this way on ivorine than it is on paper. Just take care when you remove paint with a damp brush that you do actually remove it. If it merely gets pushed to one side by the brush, you will end up with a brown scum where three colours have come together to form mud, and this spoils the look of the work. Sometimes I have used old linen over a matchstick to remove paint, so that I'm sure that the paint is actually being removed, and not just 'pushed around'.

Try to keep your washes fairly thin throughout. Some colours appear to have more gum binder in them (this seems true of the darker colours), and as you build up more strokes in darker areas, the gum starts to look unpleasant. This has always been a problem, and is noticeable even in some of the miniatures which have survived from the late sixteenth century. The dark areas look 'tacky' because of the build-up of gum. One solution may be to use tub or block colours here, instead of

Patricia Moy. 'Poppies'. Watercolour on ivorine. Image size 7 cm x 4.75 cm (2¾ in x 1⅞ in). In a private collection.

tube paint. The gum and plasticiser used in dry-cake colours differs from the combination used in tube colours, and some artists have found this to be a solution to the problem.

Your completed painting is delicate, because of the tentative hold which watercolour has on the surface of ivorine. A wet finger placed on the surface could eliminate ten hours' work. It has never been advisable to glaze the surface in any way, and if you do, I think you will be disappointed with the results. If you are pleased with your work, it's best to have it framed immediately (warning the framer, too, of the dire consequences should he place his finger on the painted surface). It is not a bad idea to place a sheet of greaseproof paper over the surface of the work, and attach the work, with a tiny spot of removable adhesive, to a clean white card. Place the work between two sheets of firm cardboard. It is safe while travelling, and while stored waiting to be framed.

CHAPTER 7
Oil on an Ivory Piano Key

Ivory was the traditional support for miniatures from 1720, and still is in many countries.

If you are keen to try ivory, search for a piano tuner. He or she will often carry a store of old keys, and may allow you to purchase some.

They will be thicker and less transparent than the ivory prepared for the miniaturist. They will only come in one size: 5 cm x 2.3 cm (2 in x 1 in) — a very awkward size — and they probably will be grubby from all those years of practice while eating a sticky bun with the other hand.

Materials Required:
Old piano keys
Old toothbrush and toothpaste (to clean the ivory)
Removable adhesive
Oil paints
Kolinsky Sable brushes (No. 3 and No. 0)
Turpentine.

The keys can be cleaned: toothpaste and an old toothbrush work wonders. Don't use too much water as the ivory may warp and crack.

When the ivory is clean and dry, attach it to a sheet of clean white paper, with a dot of removable adhesive, so that your fingers do not touch the surface again.

You can use the same colours we have discussed in watercolour notes, or you

Patricia Moy. 'East West Rocks'. Oil on ivory (piano key). Image size 5 cm x 2.3 cm (2 in x ⅞ in). In a private collection.

possibly have your own choice in oils.

I found Liquin a little too thick for my purposes, and preferred turpentine to thin the oil. (Liquin is a quick-drying medium which improves the flow of oil colours.) The paint needs to be just as thin as watercolour to work in this small area, so I still found the white palette was ideal (not the same one used for watercolour). A substitute palette could be a piece of ivorine, or, again, the plastic lid from an ice-cream container.

At first, to design in this long narrow space seems difficult. The proportions are similar to the famous 'Cigar-box Lid' series painted by the Australian impressionists in the late 1880s.

I found it easier to design within the vertical or portrait shape. It would suit a full-length figure, trees, a keyhole-type view — there are lots of possibilities when you think about it.

If the design incorporates some part of the ivory which will show through, then it will be more successful. There is really no point in working on the beautiful creamy surface in dark heavy colours.

The same two brushes, Kolinsky (Sable) No. 3, and No. 0, work well, but will need to be washed with extreme care later, if

you intend using them for watercolour again. The ideal would be to have separate brushes for each medium.

Any drawing on the surface can be done with very thin, mid-tone paint. Remember, with oil you add the lightest areas last, unless you are only working with thin transparent washes.

When you are finished, allow a few days for the paint to dry completely, in a cool dry place.

CHAPTER 8
Using Scraperboard

Tone is difficult. We feel we understand it until we try to put it into practice. I feel working with scraperboard helps, and it's fun. This board is beautifully prepared, both in France and England. The technique is borrowed from commercial artists, who use it to prepare layouts for magazines.

The board is made by superimposing a layer of an inert pigment, such as clay or whiting, bound in a glue of casein size (forming a sort of gesso) on a support of board. It can be purchased in black or white. The black board is ready to use. The white board can be painted in areas which are to be dark, with Indian ink.

The technique is not new. Artists have used graffito methods for centuries, originally scratching on cave walls. The method, when applied to miniature work, produces exquisite detail difficult to duplicate with pen and brush. By starting with black and scratching through to white, you find you must appreciate all the greys in between. You teach yourself to stipple, cross-hatch, use a fine line — or in fact any form of mark which will indicate the various degrees of grey you wish to show — so like engraving. This is all wonderful practice for later miniature painting.

Materials Required:
English scraperboard (made by Essdee), or French scraperboard (made by Canson and called Studio Grattage)
One disposable scalpel
HB pencil
Metal ruler
Stanley knife
Watercolour
Kolinsky (Sable) No. 3 brush.

A word of warning! There is no going back, and no patching is possible. If your stroke is too deep, and you dislodge the clay, the surface will look unpleasant. The idea is to move slowly and cautiously.

The black surface is very easily bruised, so if you are cutting a large sheet into small pieces, I suggest you place a sheet of paper on the board, under the metal ruler. Otherwise the pressure of the ruler will damage the surface. You will need a strong Stanley knife to cut the board.

Once you have a few small pieces, it's probably a good idea to use one to test out some strokes. See how thin that coat of black really is, and how easy it is to go too far with a stroke, and dig the clay underneath. It's vital to keep the blade sharp, so sandpaper near to hand is useful.

A black-and-white photograph from the newspaper may be a good place to start. Draw the picture with pencil on scraperboard. You could make a very graphic statement by cutting out all the areas which are not black. These areas will now represent grey and white, just like the tone drop you achieve when you photostat a colour picture.

The real enjoyment is to find your own personal calligraphy, to discover all the tones in between.

The most delicate texture can be conveyed with scraperboard. You may like to experiment with the fur of a cat, the hair of a dog or birds' feathers. By layering the strokes over and over, with slight changes in direction you can achieve a depth which is very realistic.

The finished work can be left as it is, or you can introduce watercolour if you work very slowly and gently. Because of the amount of black ink dislodged during the cutting, the scraperboard needs to be dusted lightly with a very soft brush before you introduce paint. Mix colours three times lighter than you think you will require, because they will darken considerably as they dry. Use a wash-over-wash technique, so as to gradually deepen to the tone you require.

The surface of the finished work is fairly fragile, so rush your work to the framer.

Patricia Moy. 'Just Good Friends' cut on black scraperboard. Image size 7.5 cm x 6.3 cm (3 in x 2½ in). Private collection.

Patricia Moy. 'Fertility Rite'. Cut on black scraperboard. Image size 7.5 cm x 6.3 cm (3 in x 2½ in). Private collection.

CHAPTER 9
Watercolours and White on Black Paper

This is a way of working where you need to be prepared to 'hasten slowly', and your on-work lighting needs to be excellent.

I have been working this way for years, at night. I have only recently discovered from friends who sew, which I do not, that one never works with black on black at night. I guess it makes sense, and I pass it on to you — it's too late for me.

The basic idea is to float-on washes of transparent watercolour (no white at first).

Normally transparent watercolour depends on the white paper underneath to allow it to glow. Working this way, you are depending on the black paper to act tonally on the watercolour, and deepen it, so that all your dark and shadowed areas will be depicted first as you paint. It's an odd way to paint, but I like it. When you want to depict light, as you will towards the end of your painting, you commence to add a little white to your watercolour mix. This, of course, causes the paint to become opaque, and stops the tonal effect of the underlying black.

If possible, it seems better to avoid using pure white when painting this way, and only use it when mixed with a colour. It makes such an extreme tonal jump — black to white — it often looks chalky.

The series 'William, His Life and His Times' was painted with watercolour and white on black paper.

Materials Required:
Black paper — Mi Teintes pastellist's paper — the paper needs to be sized, and not all black paper is prepared in this way
Kolinsky (Sable) No. 3 brush
Watercolours
White — Pelikan brand has been used because of its particular properties
Double water container

The black pastellist's paper comes in a sheet 75 cm x 55 cm (29½ in x 22 in). It has a highly textured side, which looks a little like mesh. This has been prepared as a 'tooth' to hold pastel. The reverse side has only a very slight texture, and this is the side which suits this watercolour technique. If you run your fingers over each side, you will be able to feel the difference. It is sometimes difficult to see it unless the light is very good.

I tend to fold the sheet in half, and cut it with a serrated knife. You can continue folding and cutting this way until you have a size slightly larger than the size you wish to work. It's a good idea not to paint right to the border of the paper, so that the framer has room for the mount without loss to your painted image.

If you are going to paint your subject and leave the black paper as a background, you could commence by blocking in its general shape in a dark transparent wash. I tend to use a complementary colour as the background wash, so that parts of it can show through after subsequent washes. So, if the final colour of the subject is to be mainly orange I may sketch the form in an Ultramarine Blue wash. As each wash dries, you can add the next one. It may take quite a few washes before the colour starts to show on the black background. I rarely pencil-in the drawing, but try to work freehand. The reason for this is that I dislike the shine which graphite leaves on the paper.

Once a colour is applied, it stains the paper, and it is almost impossible to return to the original black, so you need to work very slowly and carefully.

CHAPTER 10
Silhouettes Today

I remember a party game my parents played with visitors, when I was too young to be allowed to join in, but old enough to watch, fascinated, through the chink in my bedroom door. They would set up a table with a sheet hanging in front, and a light behind. The audience would be seated in front of the curtain. Someone would lie on the table (the patient), another two adults would be the doctor and nurse. They would commence to 'operate'. To those watching the silhouettes on the other side of the curtain, strings of sausages, hammers, knives, and all manner of things would appear to emerge from the patient's depths. The shadows were realistic, and squeals from the audience made for noisy parties.

The theatre had used silhouette long before my parents. The flat shadow puppets made their way from Asia, reaching Europe and America during the 1700s. The intricately cut shadow puppets of the Indonesian theatre are still used in performances today.

This discussion is about the painted or cut-profile silhouette, which may have developed from shadow theatre.

Some exquisite silhouettes are still displayed today in exhibitions of traditional work, in many countries. They are produced by excellent artists as beautifully as they were in the eighteenth century. But photography today is just as big a rival — bigger perhaps.

How can we enjoy playing with an authentic method, and yet make it new and exciting for the viewer of today's miniatures? Here are some suggestions:

1. Why not cut your silhouette, and place it over a freely painted background?
2. Use the area which is usually thrown away — the negative space — and place it over a free background.
3. Introduce some fine-line ink drawing behind the cut silhouette.
4. Introduce paint to the surface of parts of the silhouette itself.
5. Use gold leaf in the background, behind the silhouette, as they did in America in the early nineteenth century.

Materials Required to Cut a Silhouette:
A sheet of black Tivoli Card (215 gsm)
A disposable scalpel
A small piece of mat board
HB pencil
Acid-free glue
Background material.

Materials Required to Paint a Silhouette:
Black gouache
2 Kolinsky (Sable) brushes — No. 3 and No. 0
Hot-pressed watercolour paper
Optional: All watercolours, white gouache, gold leaf, pen, ink.

To Cut a Simple Silhouette

You need a firm but pliable black board, which will cut cleanly, and a very sharp scalpel. The disposable ones work very well.

Place your piece of black board on a piece of old mat board, or heavy-weight cardboard. I suggest you start with some very simple shapes, until you get the feel of the cut.

Draw on the shape you have chosen with a well-sharpened pencil. As you commence to cut, move the black board rather than the knife. Try not to lift the knife until you have completed the cut area. Try to return to where you commenced the cut. In this way you will not leave 'stop-start' points.

Try to cut within a border, which may be removed later if you wish. This helps to hold delicate parts together, which may tear or break if left without support during the cutting time.

Remember that it is possible to use both the negative and the positive space as a silhouette. Practice helps a lot. If you have not tried it before, you will be amazed how quickly your skill will improve.

I suggest that you use lots of subjects other than the traditional human profile. It could be birds in flight, trees at the edge of a clearing, animal shapes … Imagine how well a zebra, or a group of zebras could look. It could be geometrical shapes intertwined — imagination is the only limit.

When you have completed the cut, look at both the negative you have cut away, and the positive shape. Play with ideas on your layout pad. Maybe think about the five ideas suggested, and some of your own.

When you have prepared a background, use a thin acid-free glue, and gently paste the silhouette to your prepared area. You can highlight your silhouette with a little

Patricia Moy. 'Eye balling'. Cut silhouette on freely painted watercolour paper. Image size 14 cm x 8 cm (5½ in x 3⅛ in) — just over miniature size. In a private collection.

colour, as suggested, or you may like to highlight areas with bronze ink, or even thin white gouache. If you do use gouache, it is important to keep the layer thin, so that it looks grey rather than white. White is too great a tonal jump, and looks unattractive.

To Paint a Silhouette

You may prefer to paint a silhouette. In this case, most miniaturists would paint a very delicate outline first, and later block it in. It is the attention to fine detail, and the elegant proportions, which make an exciting silhouette. It is generally easier to paint these details in silhouette than it is to learn to cut them, but it is interesting to try both.

A SUGGESTION

Whether you wish to paint or cut your silhouette, if it is to be a profile of a person, it's an idea to take a photo of that person in profile against a well-lit window. Do as many drawings as you can, and the photographic image, which should come out black, will give you that extra assistance.

Patricia Moy. 'Afternoon Tea with Margaret'. Cut and painted silhouette placed over yellow, rose and gold leaf. Image size 10 cm x 10 cm (4 in x 4 in). With this silhouette, I have obviously been influenced by Margaret Preston (1875–1963) a well-known Australian artist whose work often involved hand-coloured woodcuts.

The still life was set up and drawn with a pencil on black Tivoli card. It was then cut with a scalpel. On a separate sheet of watercolour paper, German gilding mix was applied and, 20 minutes later, the three golds were applied in a random manner. The back of the silhouette was coated with a fine layer of the mix, and placed gently on top of the gold leaf. Colour was introduced to the surface of the silhouette in thin, transparent washes, gradually building up these washes until they became just visible. The idea was to keep the colour as low key as possible.

CHAPTER 11
Portrait

If you are interested in miniatures, then I'm sure at some time you have thought about painting a portrait. Perhaps you have tried and given up — it's not easy. But here are some steps which may help to renew your enthusiasm. I have borrowed them from the masters of the past.

Where to start? Hans Holbein is said to have always commenced with a large drawing from life. He would explore the interior form of the face, slowly and systematically. He showed, by a system of fine hatched lines, as Dürer did in his engravings, the depth of the eyes, the recession under the lower lip, the modelling of the nose. All the planes of the face were observed in careful, sensitive detail.

From this drawing, he was able to paint a large mural, or reduce to a miniature 4.6 cm (2 in) in diameter. His task was made easier by the careful drawing. He had come to know the sitter so well, and he knew his way.

We have all seen many faces throughout our lives — family, friends, acquaintances … All have two eyes, a nose, lips, ears, eyebrows and a chin, and yet we can tell them apart. We recognise each one immediately. How?

This is a good place to begin. Imagine you were going to draw a caricature of a relative or friend. Search this face. What is it that helps you recognise it from the crowd? Do the eyebrows form a distinctive pattern — are they thick and bushy or thin and angular? What about the eyelids — are they heavy and hooded, or so thin that they disappear under deepest brows? The corners of the mouth — do they turn up or down? Are the lips small and thin, or large and full? Is the nose a little longer, larger, smaller or thinner than usual? If you had to draw a quick cartoon of the person, is there a part of the face which you would exaggerate, so that they would be easily recognised?

Just before you start on that large drawing, it's worth observing the planes of the head. If you think of the head as a rectangular box, you will notice that it really has five sides. The front carries the features, each side carries an ear and hair, and hair usually covers top and back.

If you can see under the chin, then your sitter must be above your eye level, and you will be able to see up the nostrils as well (not always the most attractive viewing position). The face will be a little fore-shortened (it will be shorter in length from chin to hair line than you know it to be). You will not be able to see the inner flat edge of the lower eyelid, though you may well be able to see this area behind the upper eyelashes.

If your sitter is looking down, then once again the features and that front plane will be fore-shortened, and you will see more of the top of the head. You may not see the nostrils at all. You will probably see the inner area of the lower eyelid.

Perhaps your sitter is slightly turned away from you, a common position for portrait. It helps again to think of the head as a box. Imagine the box is turned in the same way. The long edge of the box is facing you. The part of the forehead which turns from the front to the side represents this line. The features which are furthest away from you (one eye and the lips) will appear slightly smaller as they turn away.

Proportions

Here are a few measurements which may help. They apply to an adult head, and are very general — there will always be individual differences.

1. If you were to divide the head vertically, from the top of the crown to the point of the chin (straight through the nose), and then divide this line in half horizontally, the horizontal line would dissect the eyes.
2. There is usually room for a 'third eye' between the two eyes.
3. If you draw in the eyebrows, and divide the vertical line in half between the brows and the chin, this should give you the base of the nose.
4. If you divide the area between the base of the nose and the chin into three parts, these two lines will give you the middle line of the lips, and the depression between the base of the chin and the line of the lips.
5. When viewed from the front, the ears appear to extend from the brows to the base of the nose.

If you are painting a child, the basic difference is that the first horizontal division passes through the eyebrows and not the eyes. The nose and chin are smaller, and the cheek pads are fuller. The eyes appear wider apart, and more of the iris is visible. The mouth appears more indented, and the upper lip protrudes more.

It is always a little easier to draw a portrait when you are directly in front of the sitter.

Painting in a Naive Style

The painting below has a haunting beauty. The suggestion here is not to copy the painting, but to imitate the style. (This is an original art work and the rights belong to the artist.) You may like to try this style with your own sitter.

Materials Required:
Artist quality watercolours
No. 3 and No. 0 Kolinsky Sable brushes
1 white palette
Hot-pressed watercolour paper 300 gsm
(140 lbs) and/or ivorine
Water containers.

Artist unknown. Unknown woman. Watercolour and gouache on ivory. Image size 6.2 cm x 4.7 cm (2³/₈ in x 1⁷/₈ in). In the collection of Lise Roget.

When you have completed your drawing, and you are ready to commence, wash over the whole area of the face with light skin colour. This could be a weak mix of Indian Yellow and Cadmium Red, or a weak mixture of Alizarin Crimson, Ultramarine Blue and Indian Yellow.

When it is dry, add a patch of Alizarin Crimson and Cadmium Red in a light weak mix, to define the cheeks. The same mix, but a little stronger, could be used for the lips — both upper and lower lips. The line of the lips could be the same colour mix, but stronger.

The nose is drawn in at the base with a warm brown, and a lighter shading of the same colour runs down either side of the nose.

The eyes are drawn in like two tiny ellipses, representing the upper and lower eyelashes. The lighter flat area of the lower lid could be added with the flesh colour and a small addition of white. The upper lids could be highlighted in the same way, if they are noticeable.

The shadow under the brow is a warm brown and the brows themselves are painted in firmly.

The hair is painted in as a mass, in the local or real colour, and is highlighted with white.

The background can be painted in a dark colour mixed with a little black, if you wish.

The clothes can be treated very simply, by mixing the colour you see in shadow and placing it on as a mass. The same colour can then be mixed with white, and laid over the top in areas to create reflected light.

This is a very simple, direct way to work. You will find it easy, and I think you will find it enjoyable. Don't worry that the effect is flat. This is as it should be. The style is totally naive. There has been no attempt to model the form, but I think you will find it has great charm.

A *Portrait in the Style of George Engleheart* (1752–1829)

George Engleheart was one of the great miniaturists of the late 1700s to early 1800s. He, along with Smart, Cosway and Wood, led the field.

You may like to paint your own subject in the style of Engleheart. His work is on ivory, but you could use either hot-pressed watercolour paper or ivorine. Engleheart worked in an area roughly 5 cm x 4.5 cm (2 in x 1⅝ in). This is fairly small, and you may wish to work a little larger. His format was oval. I am not suggesting that you copy his work, but that you try his style.

Assuming that you have drawn in the

George Engleheart (1752–1829). Unknown man. Watercolour on ivory. Image size 5.1 cm x 4.4 cm (2 in x 1¾ in). In the collection of A. Carney.

image in very light pencil, or painted the image outlines in very soft blue-grey, so that the lines eventually blend, you are ready to commence with the lightest wash to represent a very light skin tone. This could be a very light mix of Indian Yellow, Alizarin Crimson, and the faintest touch of Ultramarine Blue (very weak). The secret is to keep everything you do at this stage very light. You can always go darker later.

Next place in the features: the eyebrows in a slightly stronger mix of the flesh colour (this is merely to place them — it's not their final colour); the line of the lips, the shape they make when joined; the nostrils; and the upper lid of the eyes. For the area of shadow where the recess of the eye socket meets the bridge of the nose, use a light warm-brown stipple or short dry-brush stroke.

As this shadow area becomes lighter, use a pale Cobalt Blue stipple or short dry-brush stroke, which follows the form. (Engleheart used strokes not stipple, and always followed the movement of the form, in the work I examined.) Keep the lips extremely pale, particularly the lower lip — just another wash of the flesh colour you have mixed. The upper lip could be lightest Alizarin Crimson with a touch of Cobalt Blue. I cannot stress enough how pale all this must be.

Where there are areas of shadow, such as beneath the nose, under the lower lip and under the chin, try alternating strokes of Ultramarine Blue and Yellow Ochre side by side, so that to the eye it appears green. You can make your own Yellow Ochre by mixing Indian Yellow with a touch of purple — just enough to dull it. Where there are tiny creases in the skin — beneath the eye, under the cheek bone, at the corners of the mouth and in the fold of the cheek — use the palest Cobalt Blue strokes.

To complete the eyebrows, notice closely the colour of your sitter's eyebrows, and apply this colour with tiny feathery strokes.

Engleheart treated the hair very loosely, as did Cosway, with no under-colour, merely following the movement of the hair with longer strokes, in the local colour.

For white areas of clothing, Engleheart allowed the ivory to represent the mid-tone, and merely highlighted in white, and used a dark grey for the shadows. The blue jacket was washed on in its local colour, using Ultramarine Blue with a touch of white in the mix to give body. When this was dry and smooth, the artist hatched in the shadows with a blue-black mixture. It was interesting to note how loosely he treated all areas other than the face. This may have been to act as a foil for the near perfect modelling of the face.

The background used during this period was still a blue sky with clouds. I suspect, here, Engleheart used a quick wash of Cobalt Blue, with white added to it for body, placing this over the entire area of the background. When this was dry, he mixed the same blue with more white, and went over the area of blue with short diagonal strokes, allowing just a hint of the original blue to show through.

Clouds were painted in more rounded strokes of a light warm-grey (very pale). In the lower area of background, near the shoulders and arms of the sitter, he placed warm-brown strokes between the grey strokes of the clouds, to darken the tone in this area.

This is just one man's way of working, and possibly only at one stage in his painting life. We all change and develop, but it is interesting to observe the technique, and a challenge to try the method and the colours used by an artist of such stature in the world of miniatures.

William Wood (1764–1810). 'Clarissa' Dougan. Watercolour on ivory. Painted 1799. Detail only shown. (See also page 5.) In a private collection.

The Style of William Wood (1764–1810)

If you look at the detail of 'Clarissa', a miniature by William Wood, you will see another style, and you may like to experiment with it. Wood followed the form of the features of his sitter with strokes which sometimes moved over an entire area. His colours were not as adventurous as Engleheart, tending, as he did at this stage of his painting life, to use a warm brown in areas of shadow. It's interesting to see in this work by Wood, how heavily reliant many miniaturists were on the methods of the engravers.

A Contemporary Style

Another style which may inspire you can be seen in 'Sir Hugh Bidwell', the work of

Anna Partridge as a student in 1990–1991. Anna had originally studied calligraphy in England, but a move to Australia and the care of a young family had not allowed time for further painting. Late in 1990, she was persuaded by a friend to come to a miniature class. She came to learn to paint small houses, fell in love with portraits on ivorine, and has since completed five miniature portraits of her family.

At present Anna uses a stipple approach, and has restricted her use of colour in the face. As she progresses, she may experiment with stroke and colours. She has used three types of leaf to depict the robes and regalia of her brother-in-law,

Anna Partridge. 'Sir Hugh Bidwell, Lord Mayor of London 1989–90'. Watercolour and leaf on ivorine. Image size 7.5 cm x 6.4 cm (3 in x 2½ in). Frame — modern plated gold. Collection of the artist.

'Sir Hugh Bidwell': rose gold, silver and platinum. As silver will tarnish, she has coated just the silver with a fine varnish.

You can see that there are many ways of approaching portrait, and you will find the way which is most comfortable for you. It's exciting to experiment with different methods.

Tip: Compose your sitter well within your working area. If the head is placed too low, it may look as if your sitter is falling out of the frame. It's an error we tend to make when commencing portraiture.

CHAPTER 12
Gold Leaf

Gold is alloyed with copper or silver to make gold leaf. The metal is melted and moulded into a bar, and then passed through rollers until it becomes a flattened ribbon. It is then beaten into sheets that are so thin, that light can be seen through them — 0.013 mm (two-thousandth of an inch) thick.

Twenty-five of these leaves, between sheets of paper, are made into the 'book' you buy today. These are the precious leaves which have been used by the makers of icons for centuries, and more recently in Australia by Donald Friend (1915–1989) in his modern oil-on-wood panel paintings, and by Blake Twidgen (1945–   ), an artist born in New Zealand, who works with gold leaf both on top of and under oil, when he depicts rare and exotic birds and wildlife. This is to name but two. Both artists mentioned have published works and you may find it inspiring to search out examples of others. Many artists today use gold leaf in their own creative way, including printmakers who sometimes include a tiny piece somewhere in their composition. There is no reason why all the techniques applied to larger works cannot be applied to miniature work, so let's talk about laying leaf.

Materials Required:
A sheet of transfer gold leaf (rose, yellow or green)

A small jar of German gilding mix
One old brush (No. 3, small and soft)
Hot-pressed watercolour paper, or pastellist's black paper, or a gesso-coated and well-sanded wood panel
Watercolours
HB pencil

Laying Gold Leaf
It might be fun to use gold leaf with a design. Impossible — too difficult? No it's not, it just sounds terrifying. Transfer gold leaf is available from some suppliers. It can be purchased in individual sheets (loose leaf gold usually has to be purchased in books of 25 sheets).

Transfer gold has been milled so finely that it adheres to the sheet of tissue. It is more porous than loose leaf gold. Once removed from its sheet, it will float away on the lightest breeze.

It comes in three colours: yellow gold, which is 23 carats; rose gold, which has a lovely pink tinge and is 23.5 carats; and green gold, which is 16 carats.

Gold leaf is laid by painting an area with gilding mix, and then placing the gold leaf, gold-side-down, over the sized area. The gold adheres to the size, and the transfer paper is peeled away.

There are many ways to lay gold leaf, including the traditional method using gesso (prepared specially for the purpose — not acrylic gesso); gum amoniac, used when the gold is to be included in a book (gum amoniac is a resin which is soaked in water, strained and used); and the easier and quick method, using German gilding mix.

German gilding mix may stay tacky for a long period, so its use is not advised where the face of the work is to come into contact with paper (such as a book). For miniatures which will be framed under glass, this does not seem to present a problem.

GOLD LEAF FIRST — PAINT LATER
This is the golden rule. Watercolour contains gum arabic, which may retain its tackiness even when it feels dry to the touch. If you paint first and lay the gold last, you run the risk of the gold adhering to the last remnants of gum in the paint.

Laying gold leaf. The area to be gilded has been painted with gilding mix. Twenty minutes later the sheet of transfer gold leaf is placed over the tacky mix and gently pressed down. When the tissue is lifted back, gold will remain in the area where the mix has been applied. Rough edges can be tidied with an old brush.

When gold was laid by the illuminators, it was meant to look like pure sheets of solid gold. It was laid on the smoothest possible ground or base, and burnished with an agate (stone) to the highest gloss.

Gold leaf is so thin that even brush strokes can be seen underneath, so it's important the size be laid carefully, and in the thinnest layer. The mix is ready to receive the gold 20 minutes after it has been painted on the area to be gilded. It remains tacky for at least 40 hours, so there is plenty of time. It's deadly if left on the brush so it's a good idea to use your oldest brush, and wash it well in soapy water immediately after use. 'Be clean in all your doings' as Nicholas Hilliard said. Dust, hair and tissue scraps will all show through the delicate leaf.

A lot of rules, but worth it for the excitement you will feel when you successfully lay that first piece of gold. Gold leaf can be laid on watercolour paper — hot-pressed is best to achieve a smooth result, though you can lay it on medium or rough if you want texture. It can also be laid on pastellist's black paper, ivorine or gesso-prepared wood. Again, the wood needs to be sanded to a very smooth finish for best results.

STEP-BY-STEP:
1. Draw up the design with an HB pencil, and paint the gilding mix on the area where you wish to lay the gold leaf.
2. Leave for 20 minutes, or till the mix feels tacky to the touch.
3. Cut a piece of leaf (transfer sheet attached) slightly larger than the area to be gilded.
4. Place the piece of leaf directly over the prepared area, and press gently with the finger tip.
5. Peel back the tissue transfer gently.

The gold should only be in the area where the size was applied.

6. You can remove any excess gold by dusting gently around the edges with an old soft brush.

7. If the edges are still a bit ragged, you can tidy them up with a very sharp scalpel.

Note: Watercolour will take on top of gold, but only with difficulty. The surface is slippery and resists the paint. Acrylic takes with a little more ease. Oil is possibly best suited to work on the gold surface.

The initial 'A' has been gilded. How can it be used in a small painting? Where does inspiration come from?

Inspiration

Where does it come from? How do we get away from the world of 'look and put' — a situation in which many artists find themselves. They often say, 'I can only paint what I see'. In a way this is true. We are the total of all our life experiences, but sometimes these experiences have settled into our subconscious — not lost, but hidden from us. Amazingly they are still there, and still vivid, if they can be tapped and recalled.

Many years ago I read an article written by Betty Kronsky, a psychotherapist in New York who worked with artists who felt they had lost their ability to be creative. I found her suggestion a constant and unfailing source of renewal for me, and I pass it on.

She suggested when, as sometimes happens, you have an uncreative period, you use what she calls 'unconscious scanning'. Before I describe the process, I must say it just won't work if you are a very busy person who is always running to a time schedule, and never, even for a moment, able to break from that pattern. It relies on the ability to act on a whim. It does not rely on waiting for a holiday in Venice, or a painting trip to the south of France. It relies on listening to a little voice which whispers to you as you rush around doing the weekly shopping. It could happen in any of the following ways. Maybe you are buying the fodder for the week, the budget is tight and you have no intention of buying any extras; but, out of the corner of your eye, as you pass the fabric shop, you see a glint of colour which excites you.

This is exactly what has just happened to me. It was the pattern on a bolt of material and the glitter of some gold material in the window, that caught my eye. Of course I purchased a small piece of each. The excitement I felt on carrying the fabric home, and planning what I would do with it, I'm sure, justified such extravagance.

The material found in the fabric shop, which formed the original inspiration.

Unconscious scanning does not have to involve you in monetary outlay. It may happen, if you allow it, when you are taking the dog for a walk. If you allow yourself to really 'see' on that walk, instead of planning what you are going to do when the walk is over, you may notice a flower growing over a neighbour's fence. You may have passed it daily, but have never really noticed it before. Perhaps it's the way the afternoon sun is glinting on its petals at that moment. Maybe it's a white daisy, but as the late sun glows, you notice the warm lights and the cool blue-greys, and you 'see' it for the first time. You could hold that vision for your next painting. You have been doing some 'unconscious scanning'.

The miniature I am going to describe came from my experience in the fabric shop. The material is reminiscent of medieval glass windows. The gold reminds me of the gold-illuminated manuscripts. I find it amazing to think of all the ways this combination could be used, and you may think of many other ideas.

I don't want to slavishly 'copy' the

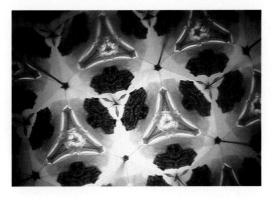

The view through the kaleidoscope. Notice how it changes design and colour percentages.

pattern or the colours of the material — it is only a springboard. By placing the material in a photostat machine, taking a copy, and then reducing it, I now have a small black and white copy, which allows

The material, black-and-white photostat, book of illuminations and kaleidoscope used to take the original inspiration in a more personal direction.

The painting which evolved: 'Where it all Began'. 10.5 cm x 8.5 cm (4⅛ in x 3⅓ in). Watercolour and watercolour with white, transfer gold leaf.

me to play with the design in my own way, using my own colours. This stops me 'stealing' another artist's work (the original fabric designer has rights), and allows me to merely use it as source material for my own invention.

Just for fun, I am going to place both pieces of material, the small black and white photostat, and a book of illuminations, on the table, and look at them through a glass-ball kaleidoscope.

This type of kaleidoscope has a glass marble at one end, instead of the more usual pieces of coloured glass. Inside the tube are three mirrors, arranged to form a multiple triangular image. It can often be purchased at newsagents and novelty stores — for colour inspiration it's marvellous. It works by breaking the image you are looking at into patterns of varying colour percentages.

With these two aids, the kaleidoscope and the photostat, you can move away from 'copying' to a world which is of your own making. The feeling of the original inspiration may remain the same.

COLOUR AS INSPIRATION

Claude Monet (1840–1926), the much-loved French impressionist, was said to have commented that when he saw a colour around him which he loved, he (metaphorically) reached out and took it, and placed it on his canvas.

Have you ever tried to work this way? It is a great joy. No initial drawing is involved — just straight to work, the inspiration coming from the first colour which takes your eye, no matter where it may be on the painted surface. It may be a patch of sunshine in the late afternoon landscape. It has a warm orange glow and you want it — take it and put it down.

Let your eye move to the colour near

the orange patch. It may well be the rich dark-green of the grass in shadow from a tree. Put it down in its shape next to the orange. Shadows often contain a hint of the complementary colour. Can you see the richness of red in the shadow? Maybe you could add this.

Patricia Moy. 'Trek to the Sunrise'. Watercolour mixed with white and flooded on black Mi Teintes paper. Image size 6.5 cm x 11.5 cm (2½ in x 4½ in). This painting just happened after a camping trip to the Flinders Ranges in South Australia. As the colour went on, the memories of a climb in the early morning to see the sunrise, came flooding back.

The idea is to keep on working this way, as if you were building a patchwork quilt of colour. If you treat each area as a shape, and match the colour as close as you can, you will be surprised at the result. You will weave a painting just as surely as you would at a loom. It will be loose, free and beautiful.

Spark A Memory

Getting in touch with memories is easier than you may think. Have you ever spent a day in a new environment, or perhaps one not experienced for quite a few years? It's been a pleasant experience, and you come home tired, warm and happy, with new images in your mind. You have taken rolls of film, and you cannot wait to have them developed. Just before they come back from the processor, you may like to try this.

On black Mi Teintes pastellist's paper, drop some watercolour mixed with white gouache — maybe two colours to commence, dividing the area into unequal parts of ⅓ x ⅔, which is a typical division for a landscape (½ x ½ divisions are usually not attractive).

While the two colours are wet, you may feel like dropping in some smaller percentages of other colours.

Watch the colours move and flow. Do you see something of your day's experience in the ways the colours are moving? It's possible that this will happen. Can you capture that fleeting glimpse of something remembered? You can push the paint around quite a bit while it is in this state. The original colours may become grey as different vibrant tints mix, but this will become background on which you can superimpose more images.

You may like to commence another while this dries. Soon you will be reliving your whole day, and the images will be your very own — not copied from photographs.

Materials Required:

Hot-pressed watercolour paper and/or black Mi Teintes pastellist's paper

Patricia Moy. 'The Maiden Aunt'. Watercolour and white on paper. Image size 12.6 cm x 5 cm (5 in x 2 in). At the time this image emerged, I was working towards an exhibition to be titled 'Nostalgia'. What is uppermost in your mind always seems to emerge when you 'drop colour' in this way.

Rotring's Gold and Silver Effect Medium
(ink)
Dr Martins inks of your choice — I like to
use the colours Chocolate Mousse,
Antelope and Olive Green — they are
more gentle
Watercolours — Artists' quality
1 good Kolinsky Sable brush (I use a
Raphael Series 8404 No. 3)
1 old No. 3 brush for ink
White gouache (I use Pelikan brand, as I
find it is the only one which will 'splat' in
the way I want it to, when added to wet
paint)
Small quantity of wax-paper
Small quantity of clear plastic food-wrap.

LET THE COLOUR FLOW

Have you ever wet an area of paper, and,
with your colours all juicy fresh on your
palette, dipped into them, and dropped
some colour on the wet receptive paper,
just allowing something to happen?

Something will happen. Immediately, if
your colour is strong and luscious, you will
be excited by the zap and flow. You will
start to see familiar shapes emerging. You
may watch fascinated, but sadly, it's too
soon. Shapes seen wet do not always stay
as the paint dries, but others do emerge
later.

Can I suggest that you wet many areas,
and flood different colours into each? After
the initial drop, don't be tempted to touch
the surface with the brush. The
intervention will be noticeable later, and
will spoil the fresh, untouched effect.

The success rate is not high. Maybe two
in ten that you are happy with, but they
are only small pieces of paper, so the cost
is not great.

There are many ways you can try this
experiment, and you will probably think of
more. Here are some suggestions, and I will

go into detail later. All are on hot-pressed
watercolour paper — except No. 6, which
is using black paper.

1. Watercolour and White Gouache
Watercolours of your choice are dropped
into an area of wet paper; Pelikan white
gouache (and only this particular white
will work) is dropped in quickly, while the
paint is still very wet.

2. Watercolour, White and Ink The
same as 1, but Dr Martins inks, in the
colours of your choice, are also added.

**3. Watercolour, White, Ink and Wax-
paper** The same as 2, but place a sheet of
crumpled wax-paper over the wet surface.
Press it down and leave to dry.

**4. Watercolour, White, Ink and Plastic
Food-wrap** The same as 2, but this time
use crumpled plastic food-wrap instead of
wax-paper. Press it down and leave to dry.
Don't be tempted to lift the paper too

*Patricia Moy. 'The Elephant and the Witch'.
Watercolour over gold effect and silver effect
medium (ink). Image size 5.5 cm x 4 cm
(2 in x 1½ in). These are the types of pattern
you are likely to see when you use crumpled
wax paper on top of the wet paint. Leave to
dry before removing.*

early, or the texture you are trying to achieve will disappear.

5. Gold and Silver Effect Medium, Watercolour, Ink and Wax-paper Using gold and silver effect medium, made by Rotring, spread the two inks in a random fashion over an area first. When the ink is dry, drop watercolour onto the surface. While this is wet, add some drops of Dr Martins ink. Cover the lot with crumpled wax-paper, and leave to dry.

6. Watercolour and White Gouache on Black Paper Use the reverse side of black Mi Teintes paper (this is the side which does not have a strong pattern). Mix some watercolours of your choice separately,

Patricia Moy. 'The Last Memory'. Watercolour mixed with white and flooded on black Mi Teintes paper. Image size 9.9 cm x 7 cm (4 in x 2¾ in).

with white, so that each is a tinted mix. Sweep these colours over a small area marked-off to a miniature size. You can intervene, to an extent, with your brush. Gouache is a little more forgiving than watercolour to this disturbance, but it too has an irritation level beyond which you proceed at your peril. It may suddenly turn 'quite plain', and become shiny and unpleasant. If applied too thickly, it will crack and fall off when dry.

It's important to remember that all inks will tend to fade in time. They are generally less light-fast than other pigments. If you are pleased with your results, and decide to frame and sell the work, it is wise to use Plexiglass, or some material which resists ultraviolet light.

I can never forget a story told me by an excellent teacher. She had sold a large painting, which had been executed in inks. She happened to visit the client many months later and was horrified to find an almost empty frame on the pleasant sunny wall of the client's home. Try it yourself some time. Paint various inks on paper, cover half of the painted area, and tape the whole sheet to a sunny window. Leave it for about 3 months, and see what happens. Sadly, inks marked 'permanent' mean, 'not immediately soluble in water', rather than that they are destined for a long life, in my experience.

One other point with ink — always use a separate brush — not your expensive Kolinsky Sable. Ink is notorious for rotting the metal ferrule of the brush, so keep an old one handy just for this purpose. Wash it out well after each use in soapy water, and rinse clean. Its life will still be short.

WHAT TO DO WITH THE RESULTS
With all these ideas the suggestion is to

look at the work when it is totally dry. Look at it from every angle — on its side and upside-down. Perhaps leave it for a few days, then take it by surprise. Often images you do not see at first will emerge. The trick is to 'tease' the image out gently, so that your intervention is not obvious.

You can just use the work as background if you wish, and paint an image on top; but I think the more successful paintings happen when you gently produce the image you have seen. Keep the palette you have used, so that when you want to mix the same colour to highlight some part of the work, it will still be on the palette. This will save time mixing and matching.

I hope this way of working sparks a memory for you.

The following series is painted in watercolour and white, on black Mi Teintes paper. The paintings are held in a private collection.

Patricia Moy. 'The Pecking Order'. Image size 7.5 cm x 8.5 cm (3 in x 3⅓ in).

Patricia Moy. 'Flopsie's Firstborn'. Image size 6.5 cm x 8 cm (2½ in x 3⅛ in).

Patricia Moy. 'Junior School'. Image size 7 cm x 8 cm (2¾ in x 3⅛ in).

Working on a Thought in Series
Materials Required:
Pastellist's black paper, or hot-pressed watercolour paper
Watercolours and brush
Pelikan White
Observation and contemplation.

We had chooks in our back garden. They were Bantams. William, the rooster, came home from the markets with his first lady, Bronwyn.

They lived happily enough, scratching around in the dust, but the egg production was pretty low, so the wives were increased: Gertrude, a skinny lass in a short skirt, Agatha, a glossy black beauty; and Flopsie, a demure hen, whose pink comb hung jauntily over one eye, came to join the couple. As seems to be the case in such polygamous relationships, they all lived happily together. No doubt due to the unstinting attention given by William to all.

They were a constant source of inspiration for me during their stay, and the reason I tell this long story is that you too may have a cat and dog, two budgerigars or maybe pet goldfish whose strong personalities you have observed. If you sit quietly for long enough and watch, even the wild birds who visit your garden will become personalities you recognise and distinguish.

Ever thought of painting a series of your observations? The series of William and his wives (depicted) comes from a time when all the females were sitting on fertile eggs. I discovered where the phrase 'hen's party' comes from, while watching them. I also liked the friendly way they set up 'play group' and 'minding sessions'.

They lived happily in our garden for many years until a clutch of eggs delivered a brood of young roosters. William, good father that he was, lined them up on the old wooden rail at 4.30 each morning and taught them to crow — not in unison, but with individual lessons. This was too much for a tightly built little neighbourhood. William, his wives and his children moved to the country.

I miss them terribly, but recently I've noticed a wild magpie in our garden. He spends hours of every day peering longingly into our large aviary, where two parrots live in splendour — I can feel another series coming on!

Finding a Miniature

Most miniaturists work in large format, and have done so for 500 years. Holbein is possibly better known today as a painter of large portraits (except by those who delight in his miniature work).

Those who do paint large paintings have surely experienced a time when the painting just does not work. Hours of work are wasted, and yet there is one small area which is glowing. You cannot bring yourself to destroy the painting because of that small area. Ever thought of turning that area into a miniature?

I can hear the critics. But why not? You are the artist. It is your ability to see that area in your work which is worth preservation, and your ability which will make that section into a complete and satisfying composition, based on your knowledge. In fact, to work this way intentionally often teaches you composition.

Materials Required:
One large unhappy painting, or one large sheet of watercolour paper
All paints (acrylic, ink, watercolour, etc.)
Kolinsky Sable brush, No. 3 and No. 0
Scissors
'L's' — two corners, cut from an old mat board frame.

In my experience, there are two distinct schools of thought in the world of art. One feels strongly that the initial conception should always be carried through to its mature image. The other allows 'the painting to take over'.

Another way to work is to commence a

painting by throwing colour paint, splatter and splash, all over a large sheet of paper, with the intention of 'finding' some small areas which delight you.

You accidentally learn about colour as well as composition. You may find that a small percentage of yellow will 'bounce' against a mass of violet; or how beautiful pale mauve can look against ochre. It's exciting.

STEP-BY-STEP
Take the two corners of the cut mat board, or 'L's', and place them on the surface of

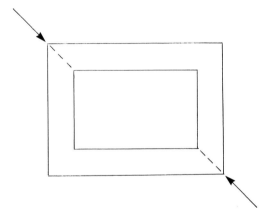

You may have an old mat board frame at home, or a framer will cut one for you. (They often have a box full of 'seconds' for you to choose from.)

the large work, increasing or descreasing the size of the opening, or framed space, as you go. Look at it from every angle until you find something you really like.

Tip: It's worth having an empty slide frame in your kit. It's useful when you are working in the landscape. You can hold it in front of you, close one eye, and 'frame' the composition you like best. Try throwing it down, at random, on the photographs in a glossy magazine. It may suggest an abstract combination of colours or design. It just might inspire you.

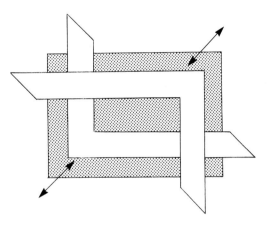

Cut the frame through the corners as indicated. You now have two 'L'-shaped pieces, and can move these over the surface of your work, changing the 'opening' as you wish — square, landscape or portrait.

CHAPTER 13
Pattern-on-Pattern Collage

Here is an idea which will help with design, colour matching, and how to mix tints and shades — all while you are having fun.

See if you can find three simple objects which have a basic shape, but differ in size and height. Two bottles and a vase have been used here. Arrange them on a table in front of your work desk, so that, as you look at them, two of the objects touch, and one remains separate (this is only a suggestion in order to keep the arrangement simple).

Materials Required:
Old glossy magazines
Layout pad
Scissors
Glue stick
Watercolours
Brush No. 3 Kolinsky Sable, with a fine point
Pencil (HB)
Watercolour paper — hot-pressed 300 gsm (140 lbs)
Mi Teintes pastellist's black paper (optional)
Pelikan White, and one tube of black watercolour (optional), if working on white paper

On a layout pad, draw up an area in the size you intend to work — 10 cm x 10 cm (4 in x 4 in), or anything smaller.

Sketch the objects as loosely as you like. The more naive the drawing the better,

It is easier to collage beside the original drawing than on top of it, so a second space has been drawn.

with this exercise. Don't try too hard for the drawing to be perfect — just let it be free.

Now, from some old glossy magazines, cut as many patterns as you can find which attract you. These could be carpet, curtain, or maybe wallpaper patterns. You may like to choose the natural pattern of a flight of birds, or animal pelt patterns, such as a striped cat. You could mix and match the two — manufactured and natural — feel free.

As it is easier to paste down large pieces first, choose two large pieces of pattern to form background and foreground. Draw up another space the same size as your drawing, and paste the background and the foreground here to cover the whole area. It is easier to place the objects on top when you are working in collage.

Now cut the shapes of the objects you have drawn, from other patterns you have chosen. Play with these and with different patterns, in different ways, until you have the colours and patterns, and a general design which you enjoy.

Sit back and look at what you have achieved. Notice that some pieces will tend to 'go back' tonally, while some will tend to 'come forward'. You can be fairly sure that the ones which recede will be patterns which contain black in the mix. The ones

which advance will probably be primary colours, or ones which have had white added to the mix.

As you arrange and rearrange your pieces, you will see how different placement improves the design. When you are satisfied, paste down all the pieces.

Hopefully you will have a collage which you would really like to paint. It will be a different arrangement to when you originally drew the objects. I hope it excites you.

If your patterns are very involved, it will take a long time, so be prepared for some detailed work — it's worth it. If you have many patterns containing black or dark tones in your collage, it may be easier to paint on pastellist's black paper (Mi Teintes). The reverse side, the side without the mesh pattern, works best.

Start with pure watercolour in the areas of pattern you perceive to be dark. The transparent watercolour over the dark paper will give you the tone you require. Add more watercolour washes to intensify the colour, but do not be tempted to add white in these areas, or you will lose the

The background, in large pieces, has been pasted down first on the second space. The choice can be made from as many smaller pieces as you wish.

ability of the black paper underneath to 'tone' your dark areas.

When you come to the light areas of pure and tinted colour, add white to your mix, but only very little at first — it is always better to 'hasten slowly' here.

It seems better not to use pure white anywhere in this design. It is too big a tonal jump from the black paper to the white paint, and often looks unpleasant. Once you use pure white, it is very difficult to remove.

If you choose to work on white, hot-pressed watercolour paper, then you will need to add black to all the colours which appear to recede (shades), and white to all the colours which appear to advance (tints) — unless they are pure primary or secondary colours (red, blue, yellow; or green, orange, purple).

It is a slow but very exciting way to work.

Patricia Moy. 'Exploring Colour'. Gouache. Image size 7.7 cm x 7 cm (3 in x 2¾ in). This painting was from another collage where no initial drawing was done. It was prepared by cutting rather naive shapes from a magazine and arranging them until satisfied. Painted on black Mi Teintes paper.

The finished collage. Image size 5.5 cm x 5.1 cm (2⅛ in x 2 in).

Patricia Moy. 'Pattern on Pattern'. Gouache. Image size 5.5 cm x 5.2 cm (2⅛ in x 2¾ in). The painting from the collage. Painted on black Mi Teintes paper.

CHAPTER 14
Painting for a Locket

English miniaturists Richard Cosway (1742–1821) and George Engleheart (1752–1829) attracted the attention of George IV of England, then Prince of Wales. Cosway was asked to paint Mrs Maria Fitzherbert, his friend, whom he later secretly married. George IV wore this miniature constantly around his neck, and when he died, at his specific request, it was buried with him.

In the days of their friendship, Engleheart was asked by the Prince to paint Mrs Fitzherbert's eye. This request started a fashion for wearing the eye of the loved one in a tiny locket. It may also have been the source of that familiar comment 'I've got my eye on you'.

Maybe you would like to paint for a small locket. Perhaps you already have a locket, or you are thinking of buying one. It's vital to have the locket before commencing the painting. It is almost impossible to buy a locket for a completed painting, and you will be disappointed if you have to trim your work to fit a locket.

Secondhand lockets can still be found, if you haunt the antique shops. Look for lockets which have convex glass (to keep the glass away from the surface of the work). These, too, can still be found if you persist. Before you make your purchase, ask to be shown how to open the locket, and how to separate the glass. Each locket opens in a different way, and can be a puzzle, and you will need to use the glass as your template.

Materials Required:
1 locket
Ivorine or hot-pressed watercolour paper
Watercolours
Kolinsky Sable brush (No. 3 and No. 0)
Pencil (HB).

When you are ready to begin painting, open your locket, remove the glass, and place it on the paper or ivorine. Trace around its outer circumference with a pencil. Remember that this measurement will be slightly larger than you want the finished work to be, because you have traced on the outside of the rim. When

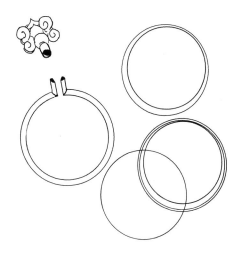

The locket has been taken apart and the glass used as a template.

you eventually cut the miniature to size, you will need to cut inside this line. I suggest that you do not make this cut until you have completed the work. If your locket is very small, there will be no place for your fingers, unless you leave the cut till last.

It may be a good idea to cut another piece of the material you are going to work on exactly to size, and try to fit it in the locket. Sometimes ivorine can be too thick for a small locket, and you would need to know this before you commence. This trial cut will also show you how much you are going to lose when you trim your painting. Place the trimmed sample over the drawing you have prepared from the glass template. Remember to keep your composition well within this area.

You are on your way to making your own personal gem.

I've painted an eye for the locket — just for fun. You may like to try painting your own eye. You will be surprised how unfamiliar you are with your own personal possession. It's great practice!

Part Four

CHAPTER 15
How Other Artists Work

Landscape

Part of the joy of the life of an artist is to be able to 'take off' into the landscape for the day, and still be 'working'. We are envied by those enclosed in air-conditioned offices. Many seek early retirement to join us. And it is a joy. To be able to sit quietly in the bush and find that the wildlife (ever present, but shy) comes to accept your presence, and even investigate you, if you are very still. You come home refreshed, rejuvenated.

These are the good days, but there are others. The rain comes, the sand swirls in biting stings, and the wind …! I once spent three hours painting a miniature out of doors on a property. Near completion, the wind blew up, whisked the small work from my hands, and had its way with it. I arrived, shame-faced, back at the homestead. Your latest work is often like a baby. You are not prepared to let go until you know it can stand on its own. I mourned its loss.

Perhaps these are the reasons many become studio artists. Time is still spent in the landscape, sketching and absorbing. This is vital. Studio time is for the expression of all that has been felt as well as seen.

Lyn Hess and Margaret Wills tend to work this way. Years spent absorbing the sight and feel of the landscape tend to emerge when they put paint to paper. Les Woollcott is inspired in a different way. He spends hours observing and photographing, then back in the studio he composes from the photographs, and delights in painting detail which cannot be seen without magnification, just as the miniaturists did, and many still do.

LYNETTE HESS

Lyn does not remember a time when she was not drawing. Inspired by watercolourist, Adelaide Perry, who was her art teacher while at school, her wish was to further her art studies. However, in the 1950s, many parents worried about their daughters entering the bohemian life of an art school, so Lyn was encouraged to take a secretarial course. As a compromise she attended night classes at Julian Ashton's Art School.

Later, Lyn became an air hostess with a national airline, an occupation which has inspired her painting life. Planes flew at 3050 m (10 000 feet) — a distance not too high to view the ground. Images are still with Lyn of vast deserts, the pale blue-green of rivers in flood, and fields of red and black Sturt's Desert Pea flowers.

Lyn is still inspired by these images. Her large works are abstractions, since she feels that the colours in nature do not always work when translated into paint. She loves

Lynette Hess. 'The Daintree'. Acrylic on board. Image size 7.4 cm x 12.4 cm (3 in x 4⅞ in). Collection of the artist.

colour and will often make her own harmonies.

Whether working large or small, she usually commences by covering the working area with one colour. Using acrylic paint, she will work into this area adding colour and constantly watching the balance of the composition. Even with her small work, she rarely uses a brush, but prefers various palette knives.

'The Daintree' was painted in this way. Commencing with one overall colour, adding more, moving it around with a palette knife, and allowing a remembered image to emerge.

LES WOOLLCOTT
Les was born in England in 1924. After working in a major London advertising studio, in 1952 he came to Sydney, for six months' holiday, and stayed.

He continued to work as a freelance commercial artist. Miniature painting commenced for him when his wife saw a miniature which she wanted in an antique shop. It was too expensive at the time, so Les decided to paint one for her. He says:

My first effort wasn't too good, but good enough to make me continue. I painted only portraits for a long time. I received lots of commissions, and had a one-man show in 'The Gallery North' in Michigan, the United States, in 1974.

In 1985, when the Australian Society of Miniature Art was formed, Les was a foundation member. He decided to paint miniature landscapes for the society's first exhibition at the Intercontinental Hotel, Sydney. He now concentrates on this type of work.

When he was four years old, he started to collect stamps. He would look at these for hours, delighting in their detail. Now

Les Woollcott. 'Mt Roland, Sheffield, Tasmania'. Watercolour on paper. Image size 4.6 cm x 5.6 cm & 3.6 cm x 4.6 cm (1⅞ in x 2¼ in & 1½ in x 1⅞ in). Collection of the artist.

Les Woollcott. 'Deloraine, Tasmania, Winter 1990'. Watercolour on paper. Image size 4 cm x 5 cm (1½ in x 2 in). Collection of the artist.

he delights in painting the same detail in his miniature landscapes, details which can only be seen with the aid of a magnifying glass.

Les works from his own photographs, masking off areas, and creating his own compositions, sometimes finding two or more miniatures in the one photograph.

He has used the same box of Schmincke watercolours for 20 years. He works on hot-pressed watercolour paper, with two brushes: No. 00 and No. 2, Series 7. He always masks off the area where he is going to work with tape, so that he can work freely, then remove the tape and have crisp clean edges.

Now living in Tasmania, Les finds it an ideal place for painters. 'Lots of mountains and trees, four definite seasons, and terrific cloud effects', he claims.

Like so many miniaturists, he also works with pastel in large format. Here he feels he can really let himself go. He can stand back and look at them from a distance,

instead of 'being hunched up over a table with a double zero brush in my hand'. I'm sure he is right. The two methods of working, large pastel and small miniature, are such a good contrast — physically and emotionally.

MARGARET WILLS
Born in 1933 in Cape Bauer, Streaky Bay, South Australia, Margaret Wills knows she is returning, in her paintings, to the scenic texture and feel of her childhood.

Margaret remembers watching whales at play, exploring the vast cliffs and sand dunes, but most of all she remembers the 'muck and grot'; the tangle of exposed roots blown free from the sand by the constant wind; the texture of the wave-lashed rocks.

It's this 'muck and grot', as she so colourfully describes it, that she returns to in her painting, and which she feels is so typical of the Australian landscape. She points out that even the snow fields of Mt Kosciusko in New South Wales, because of their comparatively low height by European standards, contain low stubbly

An old plastic container has been filled with water. A spray container of high-gloss enamel (black) is held at an angle to the tray, and the paint is applied in short 'spits' to the surface of the water. This is important. A steady stream will not give the same textured pattern.

It is important to work quickly now, because the paint dries quickly on the surface of the water. A piece of watercolour paper (any grade and any weight) is cut slightly smaller than the surface area of the water container. This paper is a medium-grade paper which has a slight texture (cold-pressed). The paper must be dry — if not, the enamel will lift off. This paper is held in both hands and slightly bowed. In this position it is gently lowered onto the surface of the water and submerged. It is lifted off quickly and placed, face-up, to dry. (Later it is worth looking at the reverse side — sometimes it may also have an interesting pattern.)

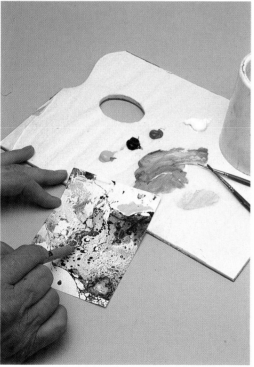

The textured pattern should be left for a few days to ensure that the enamel is totally dry. Using the fine waterproof pen, slight adjustments are made to some areas. The pen is used on the side to prevent making dark marks.

Margaret Wills, mixed media, step-by-step.

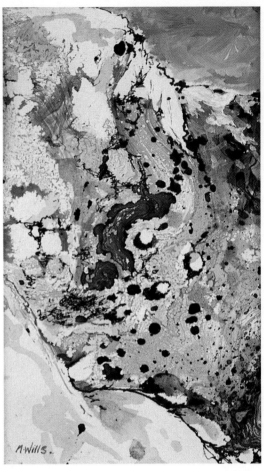

Using acrylic paints, an opaque mixture of mauve-grey is mixed using all colours except black. This is painted into the area which will become sky. Margaret has decided that the textures produced remind her of areas of the Snowy Mountains in New South Wales, so she will continue to work on details of the pattern to produce this memory.

Using the same mix of three colours, without white so that the mix is transparent, the painting continues over the areas of texture. Transparent blue is used for the shadows on the snow.

Once the painting is finished, it only remains to be signed. This needs to be done under magnification to be in keeping with a small work.

Margaret Wills, 'Snowy Mountains Blizzard'. Image size 12 cm x 7 cm (4¾ in x 2¾ in).

growth and lichen-covered rocks sprinkled throughout and up to their highest peaks.

Margaret studied watercolour in Adelaide, and later, after marriage and a move to Sydney with her family, she enrolled at the Royal Art Society, where she continued her studies in portraiture with Garrett Kingsley, and in landscape with J. Lindsey Sever.

Later, Marion Farley was to introduce her to the struggle which is sincere abstraction. Margaret continued applying the same rules she had been taught in traditional work, but dragging a response from her creative emotions. It gave her a healthy respect for the work of the abstractionist.

Margaret works and teaches in a big airy studio built in the grounds of her own home. From her work and her teaching, she has found that students find it easier to paint realistic perfection than to express an emotional response to the landscape.

She feels some artists' morality restricts their view of the world, and, sometimes, the time they feel 'permitted' to 'waste' — time which is viewed as selfish because it cuts out the rest of the world. There is often pressure to produce a work which gains immediate approval of others, in order to compensate for this time which is considered 'wasted'.

Margaret feels it is important that the students be given time to develop in their own way. Given materials and techniques, and with time to feel good about themselves, students find the way which is right for them.

Materials Required:
High-gloss enamel spray can (Margaret is using black, but you could use brown and/ or silver, or any other colours of your choice)
Acrylic paint — A20 Yellow Medium, Ultramarine, Bright Red, Black and Titanium White were used
Pen — Waterproof, fine, black
Brushes — No. 000 and No. 2 Sable, and a Series 70 large (mixture of squirrel and sable)
Palette — An old plate, or a disposable paper palette
Water container for dip — An old 'throw away' plastic container

Water container to wash brushes
Watercolour paper — Any grade and any weight. Different grades will produce different results.

Tip: If you spread a sheet of greaseproof paper over a wet sponge, and place it in a large plastic tray with a lid (often used to store meat), you can use this as an excellent 'throw away' palette for acrylic. The acrylic does not dry as quickly, and when it does, you merely throw the greaseproof paper away and replace the sheet.

Figurative

Attending life class has always been a very important part of an artist's training. Many working artists continue the practice, on a weekly basis, for the rest of their lives, knowing that the knowledge they gain flows into all areas of their work. A short pose trains the artist's eye to grasp the essential line or movement. A long pose allows detailed study of the form, just as in landscape. The work of Australian artist, Brett Whiteley, clearly shows his years of study from the model. His landscapes always show the same rhythmic form he has observed in the figure.

Two artists who use the figure directly in their large and miniature work are Madeleine Szymanski and Erika Beck. Madeleine studies the form carefully in her watercolours, sometimes using images from the past, but often making direct comment on the dress and attitudes of today. In her work as a printmaker, she incorporates the figure and weaves it into a composition of colour and texture, making a strong contemporary statement.

Erika takes the rapid poses from life class studies, and weaves them into a musical composition full of rhythm and

For this watercolour Madeleine Szymanski has drawn the image using a 2B pencil on Arches hot-pressed watercolour paper 300 gsm (140 lb). The edges have been masked with removable tape to ensure they will be crisp when the painting is completed.

Madeleine uses artist quality watercolour and her palette for this painting consists of Ultramarine Blue, Raw and Burnt Sienna, Burnt Umber and Permanent Rose. Her brushes are No. 2, 1 and 00 Kolinsky Sable. Madeleine works in watercolour washes from light tones to darker tones, gently deepening the colours.

Masking fluid is painted in small areas where she wishes to retain white paper. This solution is waterproof when dry and acts as a block out. It can be rubbed off when the painting is completed. The small plant fibre Madeleine is using is from the paper bark tree. She discovered its use when she was searching for different textures for her collagraphic plates. Now she finds that the fine fibres are ideal for applying masking fluid to delicate areas. The fibres have the added advantage of being disposable (masking fluid destroys brushes if not washed off immediately). Pine needles could possibly be used in the same way.

Madeleine Szymanski,
watercolour, step-by-step.

Madeleine Szymanski, 'Sylvie Sewing'.
8.4 cm x 6.2 cm (3¹/₃ in x 2³/₈ in).

movement. Her large acrylic studies, and her miniatures in watercolour and gouache, echo this wish for freedom and life.

MADELEINE SZYMANSKI

Since Madeleine commenced presenting her work in competitive exhibitions in 1988, she has received an avalanche of awards for her watercolours, prints and miniatures. In 1990 alone, she was awarded first prize in 12 competitions.

In all her work, she tends to favour the human figure. As she says:

My basic interest is in portraying people. I like the design possibilities inherent in the shapes of the human figure. I like the challenge involved in drawing figures accurately and with naturalness, so that the viewer can identify with them. I want to make pictures that communicate honest feelings and emotions, and which will validate common human experience. I would like to think that my work might inspire a recognition of the essential spiritual unity which is shared by all human beings.

Her large-format and miniature watercolours are usually gentle and traditional, carried out in a series of everdeepening washes. Her prints, though still featuring the figure, are often more contemporary in approach.

Originally trained as a teacher, with an Art major, Madeleine came to use watercolour for post-graduate study. Working constantly with the medium, she feels it is most seductive. She loves the excitement of the paint being a little out of control. She loves the element of risk, not available in oil or acrylic for her.

Having attended life class for many years, she feels confident to refer to old family photographs, sometimes sepia or black and white, adding, subtracting, and making changes as she wishes.

In her watercolour miniature 'A Summer Day', Madeleine has used hotpressed Arches paper (300 gsm/140 lbs). Starting with the lightest tone, she has gradually added washes to deepen the tone. Areas of light are represented by white paper.

In her second watercolour, "Sylvie Sewing", Madeleine demonstrates her working method.

Her third figurative work, 'Seachild', is a collagraphic print (a collagraphic plate is made from a carefully prepared, raised collage, then a print is taken). She has

Madeleine Szymanski. 'A Summer Day'.
Watercolour on hot-pressed paper. Image size
8 cm x 8 cm (3¹/₈ in x 3¹/₈ in).
Private collection.

Madeleine Szymanski. 'Seachild'. Collagraph
printed on German etching paper. Image size
11.2 cm x 8 cm (4³/₈ in x 3¹/₈ in).

made the plate for this print by attaching
fine vilene to a small piece of mat board.
She has pulled delicate threads from silk
organza, and attempted to arrange them in
the form she wishes, though she comments
that these threads lead a life of their own,
and tend to be 'a little out of control'. She
uses gloss acrylic medium to place them in
position, and coats the whole plate with a
very thin wash of the same medium. The
advantage with this medium is that it dries
quickly. If too much is used, it will clog the
fabric of the vilene, and weaken the
strength of the print.

Printing methods today allow
experimentation and creativity, and
Madeleine uses the medium to great
advantage in her contemporary work, both
large and small.

ERIKA BECK

Erika is well known for her large, often
figurative work. She says: 'It is based on
artistic intuition, rather than current
trends. It draws its strength from the
individual and particular expression of
personal experience of life'. She describes
her style as 'figurative expressionism', and
goes on to say:

I do not feel particularly tied to so-called
'reality', the external appearances not being of
primary importance. I believe very strongly
that art does not reproduce what is visible — it
makes visible. I manipulate colour in the same
way musicians manipulate the notes in a fugue

Erika Beck. 'Bathers Playing'. Watercolour and gouache on paper. Image size 8.5 cm x 11 cm (3¹/₃ in x 4³/₈ in). Collection of the artist.

— in colour phrases. I tend to defuse objective images into colour plates and rhythms.

She finds her inspiration comes from everyday experiences of people and objects — nature and events touch her in a personal way.

Erika may start painting by playing with colour, responding to it spontaneously. As

Erika Beck. 'Oberon'. Watercolour on paper. Image size 8 cm x 10.5 cm (3¹/₈ in x 4¹/₈ in). Collection of the artist.

Erika Beck. 'Lilies'. Watercolour and ink on paper. Image size 10.9 cm x 8.7 cm (4¹/₄ in x 3³/₈ in). Private collection.

she proceeds, she may find that the painting requires the experience of a new object, and so the painting grows. She feels that the best painting has to 'happen'. It happens to you, and you express this visual experience and communicate with others.

Having recently held a successful solo exhibition based on her large work, Erika has returned briefly to miniature, saying that she feels the small size provides a personal visual experience, 'Like pillow talk with a lover'.

Still Life and Flowers

After many years of training, working and teaching, many artists feel, as do Janine Bravery and Judith Buist, that they do not wish to compete with photography. They

85

prefer to bring an expression of themselves to their art. Both artists have 'taken in' many visual effects from other associated fields of work. Janine, from her years of weaving, expresses, almost unconsciously, the desire to achieve texture, colour and design in her paintings, both large and miniature. Her present collagraphic plates successfully demonstrate this search. Similarly, Judith, after years of fine line-work and etching, was exposed to an intense period of work with related disciplines. Handmade paper, machine embroidery and porcelain presented mediums which she could incorporate into her etching, pastel and watercolour. The combination has become a very personal expression.

JUDITH BUIST

After working for twenty years as a freelance commercial artist, Judith studied etching for three years with Elizabeth Rooney, at the Willoughby Workshop Art Centre, Sydney, and continued this study with Jenny Pollack. Her interest then extended into woodcut and lino print, with Ruth Burgess. When she wished to explore two-colour, one-plate printing, she attended classes with teacher Gweneth Wood, at Ku-ring-gai Art Centre (Sydney). Here she was introduced to collagraphs. She stayed on, finally taking the class herself for 12 months, when Gweneth became ill.

During this period, a term of experimental workshops was offered at the centre — a unique idea proposed by the centre manager, Gloria Allport. A teacher from each discipline at the centre was to teach two sessions during the term. Those attending were exposed to paper-making, porcelain doll making, machine embroidery and quilting. Many were artists whose tools had previously been paint and paper.

Judith Buist. 'Landscape with Waratah'.
Etching with pastel and watercolour. Image size
9 cm x 8 cm (3½ in x 3⅛ in).

Judith Buist. 'Patchwork Environment'.
Etching with pastel and stitching. Image size
8.5 cm x 8.5 cm (3⅓ in x 3⅓ in).

Suddenly they were encouraged to explore the possibilities of incorporating all or any of these new materials and methods, into their own work.

For Judith, this was a turning point.

She found that by combining the paper she was now able to make by hand, with some embroidery stitches, maybe a small appliqué, an impression of her etched plate, and perhaps some fine line-drawing or pastel additions, she could produce an expression which was uniquely her own.

She went on to make porcelain dolls, but knows that she will eventually incorporate parts of the porcelain itself into the mixed media work she is now producing.

Like other artists, Judith works in large format as well, and has received two important awards for a major works using many of these materials in combination.

Judith feels many artists are looking to combine materials in different ways today, and wonders if this is 'an expression of the sensory overload we are experiencing in life, so full of multiple images'.

Collage, once thought of as play, is now considered and accepted as an art form in its own right.

No longer interested in producing editions of her etchings, Judith prefers to produce an original piece without repetition. She is constantly inspired by the diversity of nature. She is aware of the tiny seed pods and flowers, which are often overlooked, and yet contain a richness of decoration, sometimes unmatched by larger varieties.

Judith is aiming for work which is different and compelling. Her wish is to involve the viewer, so that they may stop and think. And her wish is being granted.

Judith often prepares small etchings (about

Judith Buist. 'Christmas'. Collagraph with pastel drawing and stitching. Image size 10 cm x 7 cm (4 in x 2¾ in).

10 cm x 14 cm) (4 in x 5½ in) on zinc plates. These may be traditional landscapes, or any other subject she chooses. Sometimes she may not be happy with the result when the plate is printed. As so often happens, there may be areas which are working and some which are not. She looks carefully at the print, and cuts it into the smaller pieces she wishes to keep. These she rearranges to form a pleasing abstract pattern.

When satisfied with the new design and the parts she has selected, she cuts the plate into the same pieces, and prints them in the new arrangement. It rarely works if small parts of different plates are mixed. In order to carry through a feeling, the small pieces need to have come from the one master plate.

Sometimes combining a fine line-drawing of a wildflower, Judith may cross and intertwine the drawing with the print. Later she might introduce the coloured line of a pastel pencil, maybe a little watercolour, and perhaps a finishing touch with a soft pastel to complete the work.

Growing native wildflowers in her own garden, Judith uses these, sometimes waiting months for a special flower to bloom so that she can complete an idea. She dislikes working from photographs, preferring the stimulation of reality.

Though she sometimes commences by drawing a native flower in detail, she feels the flower needs a landscape, and this is how her present series has developed.

JANINE BRAVERY

Artist, teacher and Founder/President of the Australian Society of Miniature Art, Janine Bravery works in many mediums in a contemporary manner. Five years ago, she began etching but found that her search was for colour and texture. When collagraphs were introduced she was immediately interested. Janine has printed from the collagraphic plate for a few years now, but has only recently realised that the plate has an intrinsic beauty of its own. She now presents the plate itself as the finished miniature. With the acceptance worldwide of such a broad field in the work of miniaturists, the presentation of a collagraphic plate adds yet another dimension to the world of art.

Janine works with board, watercolour paper, dish wipes, raffia, grit, thread, nylon mesh, wool ... any material which will provide texture.

She begins with a sheet of acid-free mat board, and draws her image directly onto

Janine Bravery. 'Homage to Van Gogh'. Collagraphic plate, using dish wipes, grit and thread to form texture. Image size 10 cm x 7.5 cm (4 in x 3 in). Collection of the artist.

it. Sometimes she will trace this image, and transfer it to rough or medium-textured watercolour paper. This image is cut out with scissors or a Stanley knife.

Now the mat board is coated with PVA glue, and when it is tacky, the cut images are pressed down on top of the original design. Pieces of thread, cloth, sand ... anything may be added at this stage to form a textured surface. (This is where Janine has found that her approach is slightly different from making a collagraphic plate for printing. She is choosing not only the texture, but also the colour of the pieces she is adding.)

The plate is left to dry completely, and then given a second coat of glue.

Janine may still ink up the plate and take a print, but if she intends to use the plate as her miniature, she will use oil paint mixed with Liquin rubbed into the textures of the plate. This will add colour in much the same way as when the plate is inked up ready to print.

It would seem that the plates Janine is currently producing are a culmination of her years as a weaver, painter and teacher. She feels she always sees pattern strongly, then colour, tone and texture. As a weaver she preferred to take her own wool 'from the sheep's back' and spin it herself. Her memories are of a strong tactile sense, even as a very young child.

Today, the elements which excite her to paint are still tactile. The rough feel of hand-made paper — the shape and texture of sea weed, shells and sand. She is not interested in traditional work, feeling that a camera can do this quite well. She feels that in non-traditional work, painting becomes an expression of oneself, and this is her aim.

Abstract
Stuart Cole has enjoyed working with pastel in miniature for many years. He works with many layers of hard pastel on

Stuart Cole. Untitled. Pastel on mat board.
Image size 10 cm x 10 cm (4 in x 4 in).
Courtesy Eaglehawke Galleries.

Alpha mat, an archival mat board used in framing. His small works are often a preparation or thinking process for his large oils or acrylics.

He starts in a small area, placing layer on top of layer. He may divide the space up into unequal proportions, or he may treat it as a whole. The base layers become subdued as they mix and become tertiary colours.

On top of this tertiary base, Stuart often bounces his tiny images, which usually carry primary colours. These images may be in the form of a straight or curved line, a small dot or an elongated shape. No matter what shape they take, they add movement and excitement.

Stuart sees all his works as totally abstract. They are reminiscent of the work of the abstract expressionists who, in their action paintings, used paint manipulated in various ways to create space which would involve the viewer. Natural forms were simplified or rejected, and colours were arranged in a way which aroused emotion.

Part Five

Preservation and Care

Perhaps you have a treasured miniature, or are considering a purchase. The fact that miniatures can still be seen which were painted over 500 years ago is a tribute to their custodians and, in many instances, to the hours of attention given them by devoted conservators.

Karen Coote, B.A. (Sydney), B.Sc. (London), is an archaeological conservator. Originally trained as a jeweller, she is currently senior conservator at the Australian Museum, Sydney. She has restored miniatures in private collections, and for the National Gallery, Canberra.

For those entrusted with the care of a miniature, she has passed on the following advice.

The two greatest enemies of the miniature are excessive exposure to light and extreme humidity. Exposure to light will fade the delicate watercolour. Humidity may warp the support, especially if that support is ivory.

Mould and dust can appear on the most perfectly sealed miniature. In time, paper products and glue, used in the backing inside the case, will break down. Fine particles of these items migrate to the surface of the painting, and are often visible through the glass.

Karen suggests that a miniature should only be unsealed when there is a genuine need. This could be for the removal of mould, powdery and flaking paint, or dust.

Albin Roberts Burt (1783–1842). 'Mr Grimshaw'. Watercolour on ivory. Painted 1813. Image size 6.5 cm x 5.4 cm (2½ in x 2 in). Private collection.

A poor attempt has been made to restore the paint area of the background near the profile. The new paint will be removed carefully with the aid of a binocular microscope. Restoration can then take place.

She stresses that this operation should not be entrusted to anyone who is not aware of the pitfalls.

If dismounting is to take place, it must be in a controlled environment. A change in humidity may cause ivory to buckle, and

Detail of the miniature 'Mr Grimshaw', showing the technique of the artist and poor restoration.

it may never return to its original shape.

There is no standard methodology in the assemblage of the various parts of the frame. Each one differs. It would be wise to consult a jeweller, and to record the methodology when opening a case, so that the parts can be replaced with ease, and in the correct order.

Sometimes there will be paper, or a paper product backing, behind the ivory. This may have information supplied by the artist. If the paper has deteriorated it may have to be discarded. Make sure that this information is recorded and, if possible, a photostat copy made.

Often the ivory will be sealed to the paper product backing with gold beaters' skin and, perhaps, rabbit-skin glue (sealing together outer edges of ivory and paper). There may be multiple layers of paper which act as a buffer zone and absorb moisture. None should be removed unless absolutely necessary.

Sometimes the artist may have painted on the reverse side of the ivory. This paint should not be removed.

In works where severe damage has taken place, a decision may have to be made. If the integrity of the piece cannot be preserved, for instance, if the features of the face, the most important part of a portrait, are lost, then, ethically, restoration could not take place.

Any work to be done should only be carried out by an expert, and only under a binocular microscope. Conservation and restoration are delicate, and highly skilled operations. Make sure you consult a specialist.

The First Miniaturists in Australia

There have been artists, both amateur and professional, who have worked in Australia since settlement in 1788. Some came as convicts (sometimes transported for forgery), some settled freely, and eventually many were born in the country. Just as artists today, they were versatile. Many were known for their larger work, but they were also miniaturists.

The First Fleet arrived in Botany Bay in 1788. On board one of the transports of the First Fleet, the FRIENDSHIP, was Lieutenant Ralph Clark, who recorded in his diary, 'Kist your dear image as usual on this day and read the prayers'. The image referred to was a small portrait of his wife, Betsy Alicia, waiting for him at home in England. Now held in the Mitchell Library, it was perhaps the first miniature painting to arrive in Australia.

Many more miniatures were to arrive in the baggage of those who, for various reasons, had decided to come as soldiers or free settlers to a new land. Some of the more affluent visited the miniaturist before they embarked. The freshly painted miniature would be given to the family who was left behind — perhaps with a tiny lock of hair, carefully woven and locked into the back of the case. When the remaining family joined the new settler in the adopted country, these miniatures, often painted by leading miniaturists of the day, would also come to settle in Australia. Examples of the work of Smart, Cosway,

Engleheart, Wood and others found their way to Australia, as they did to other countries, and some still reside here in public and private collections.

It wasn't long before artists too were joining in the migration. By September 1808 the *Sydney Gazette* carried an advertisement for John William Lewin, stating that he would execute miniatures for five guineas and portraits for forty shillings. As miniaturists rarely signed their work, it has proven extremely difficult to verify work by many of the early artists who now followed in succession.

In 1842, the first daguerreotype was taken in Sydney. The original little portraits taken this way measured 8 cm x 5 cm (3 in x 2 in), and were often hand-coloured, sometimes by the miniaturists whose existence was threatened by the new invention.

By 1880, outdoor landscape photography was possible because there had been a technological breakthrough. By 1900, anyone could purchase a roll of film and a box Brownie camera, and set off to record their own world. Both forms of miniature were now threatened — portrait and subject. Some artists continued, but the majority of the historical work which has survived comes from the period 1788–1900. Miniaturists from the period 1900 to the present day have not been documented in any detail.

A Selective List of Australian Miniaturists

Born–Died	Artist	Arrived in Australia
	Allen, Josiah	
1806–1895	Allport, Mary Morton	1831
1813–1895	Backler, Joseph	1832
1801–1861	Becker, Ludwig	1851
1813–c. 1899	Berkeley, Martha	1847
1790–1855	Bock, Thomas	1824
1887–?	Brookes, Daisy M.	1915
	Butterworth, Margaret	
	Clayton, Samuel	
	East, T. B. or J. B.	
	Edgar, Edmund	1826
1880–1962	Edwell, Bernice	(as a child)
	Elyard, Samuel	
1868–1961	Gibson, Bessie	(born in Queensland)
	Golding, Bess	
1817–1903	Horsley, J. C.	
	Ireland, Beryl	
1868–1960	Kong Sing, Justine	
	Laycock, Gladys	
1805–1890	McCrae, Georgiana	1841
1888–?	Marks, Stella Lewis	
	Meredith, Louisa Ann	1839
1809–1854	Nicholas, William	1836
	Ramsden, Richard H.	
1765?–?	Read, Richard, Senior	1813
1796–1862	Read, Richard, Junior	1819
	Reid, Edward	
1802–1860	Rodius, Charles	1829
1812–1894	Stephen, George Milner	(as a child)
1878–1939	Tait (Norris), Bess	(born in Victoria)
1807–1876	Walker (Chauncey), Theresa	1837
1858–?	Whiting, Ada	

Compiled from information available at the time of writing.

It takes considerable research, beyond the discussions here, to name the many artists of that period. Often work was not signed and can only be verified by an expert examination of style.

At the time of writing, although the history of the Australian miniature has been researched by an authority on the subject, the work is, as yet, unpublished.

Galleries, libraries and museums in all states have collections, large and small. Some collect with an eye to the work of a particular artist, others collect on the basis of the historical relevance of the sitter, as is the case with the collection housed at the Mitchell Library, Sydney. Styles vary from those trained in traditional methods of the Royal Academy, London to the most naive work of talented convicts.

The traditional work is carried out in watercolour on ivory, but a variety of examples exist, from the work of an excellent wax modeller, a carver of kerosene shale, to exquisite landscapes painted in oil on gumleaves.

The list on the preceding page is offered merely as a starting point to anyone who would wish to explore further, knowing well that many names may, and I'm sure have, escaped these tentative efforts.

Richard Read (senior) (1765?–?) arrived as a convict on the EARL SPENCER in October 1813. He was about 48 years of age, and had been transported for having been found with forged notes in his possession. He quickly gained his ticket-of-leave, and by 1814 had set up a business at 37 Pitt St, Sydney, where he ran a school, painted miniatures and offered designs for embroidery and needlework for sale. He promised to teach the 'polite and elegant Art of drawing in its most elevated form'.

Read's style with watercolour was to use extensive stipple in the background, loose treatment of the clothes, and attention to detail with the facial features. He claimed to have been taught by Sir Joshua Reynolds, but there is some doubt about this claim.

Read built up a clientele of important government officials and their wives, and the ever-growing group of prosperous merchants. Among miniatures he is known to have painted were portraits of Governor Lachlan Macquarie and his wife, and a rather haunting image of their young son,

which is held in the collection of the Mitchell Library (though the attribution has not been verified).

Read was pardoned in 1826, and appears to have left Australia at that time. It would seem that he returned to England via Tahiti, where he is believed to have painted birds now in the collection of the Royal Commonwealth Society, London.

Next to advertise in the *Sydney Gazette* in 1817 was **Josiah Allen**. He was still listed as a miniature painter in the Post Office Directory in 1832. **Samuel Clayton**, in his early advertisement, promised he had 'now ready for practice a much improved and systematic machine for taking Likness in profile on a most correct principal and in a few minutes, at ten shillings each'. This is evidence of perhaps the first silhouettes being made in Australia.

To confuse the small population, a second artist, a free settler named **Richard Read**, arrived in the colony in 1819. Read Junior had his residence at 59 Pitt Street, Sydney, where he taught and painted miniatures. The first Richard Read quickly added 'Senior' to his name; the younger, newer arrival added 'Junior', and asked his clients to observe that he had no connection with any other person of the same name. It has now been proven, by family research, that the two were father and son.

Read Junior moved a number of times, but appears to have remained in Sydney till at least 1849, when there is record of his work in an exhibition. His price for a miniature on ivory in 1833 was five guineas. He moved to Victoria towards the end of his life, and died there in 1862.

In Tasmania, **Thomas Bock** (1790–1855) had arrived aboard the ASIA in 1824. He too was a convict and had been transported for having administered drugs to procure an abortion. His sentence was 14 years. He was an accomplished artist and quickly found work in the production of the first Van Diemen's Land banknotes. He received his pardon eight years later in 1832.

Bock had the ability to achieve the character of his sitter. His lithographs, large paintings and miniatures are extremely sensitive. He usually made a large pencil and crayon sketch before commencing his portrait, and when these are examined, the style is very similar to the detailed work of the English miniaturist William Wood (1768–1809). The hatched lines in the shadowed areas of the face follow the same rhythmic pattern as they flow over the underlying form.

Bock was one of the few portrait and miniature artists who was not threatened by the advent of photography, but rather embraced it, seeing in this new medium endless possibilities. His works have survived and are now represented in the Allport Library, Hobart, and in the Mitchell and Dixson Libraries, Sydney.

George Milner Stephen (1812–1894), who had arrived in Sydney as a child, was educated at Sydney College (now Sydney Grammar) and went to Hobart in 1833 as a newly appointed clerk in the Supreme Court. He led a multi-faceted life, moving between New South Wales, South Australia and Victoria. Painting miniatures was only a very small part of a life which saw him as Advocate General of South Australia, sitting member of the Legislative Assembly for Collingwood, and manager of the British Australian Gold Mining Company. Later he became a faith healer and was said to have treated the Prince of Wales. One wonders when he found time to paint.

In 1829 a young man arrived in Sydney as a convict. He had been charged with stealing a smelling bottle, an opera glass, a handkerchief, no doubt the contents of a silk bag, which he also stole. He was **Charles Rodius** (1802–1860). He had been trained as an architectural draughtsman, so he soon became drawing tutor to the children of Chief Justice Francis Forbes. Though he painted miniatures, his style was a little in the nature of caricature.

Mary Morton Allport arrived in Tasmania with her husband in 1831, from England. By July 1832 she was advertising that she intended to paint or copy miniatures: ten guineas for originals, five guineas for copies. Her portraits were a little naive, but her flower and insect studies were excellent. Some of her work can be seen in the Allport Library and Museum of Fine Arts, State Library of Tasmania. She painted a miniature of friend and fellow artist, John Glover, which is in the Allport collection.

Already another forger had been transported to New South Wales, landing in Sydney in May 1832. **Joseph Backler** was said to have had good education but lacked 'benefit from paternal oversight or example'. He was born in 1813, and was only 19 when he was sentenced to death, but this was commuted to transportation for life. After spending time in Port Macquarie, he returned to Sydney with his ticket-of-leave in 1843. He started his business advertising moderate terms for his portraits, miniatures and landscapes in oils and watercolours. He died at the age of 82, in 1895.

William Nicholas (1809–1854) arrived as a trained engraver and lithographer, in 1836. He was a free settler and, according to the *Sydney Morning Herald* of June 1847, he was 'one of those quiet unobtrusive men of genius who work their way into notice and distinction without any assistance from the newspapers'.

A painting exists by Nicholas which is slightly larger than miniature, but still executed in the miniature technique. It is of Mrs John Macarthur (Elizabeth Macarthur of Elizabeth Farm, Parramatta) as an elderly lady, and the treatment is very tender. He was equally adept at depicting young ladies.

Ludwig Becker (1808–1861), a multi-talented man, arrived in Launceston, Tasmania, in 1851. Born in Darmstadt, Germany, in 1808, he fled the revolution in his country in 1848, and after spending time in Rio de Janeiro, he headed for Tasmania. He began painting miniatures and was quickly accepted into the society of the day. The Governor, Sir William Denison, was to write this of him:

He is one of those universal geniuses, who can do anything; is a very good naturalist, geologist, etc. and draws and plays and sings. He is travelling this country and pays his way by drawing likenesses — miniatures, which he does very nicely indeed. He is very odd looking with a large red beard.

A self-portrait in the La Trobe Library, Victoria, attributed to him, actually shows him to be a handsome man in his mid-forties, with no beard but a long moustache.

He was a lithographer and a skilled portrait artist, as well as a fine miniaturist with an ability to convey character.

When the expedition of Burke and Wills was being mounted to explore the interior of Australia in 1860, Becker, ever the adventurer, applied to join the team as artist, naturalist and geologist. Although he was 52, he was accepted.

The party suffered terrible privations on this journey, and Becker perished, along with others at Bulloo, south of Coopers Creek, in April 1861.

Governor Denison's references to Becker were not exaggerated. Becker was one of the earliest authorities on the lyrebird, and he left behind drawings, scientific notes and diaries which are some of the best records of this historic expedition to survive.

One of his miniatures has been restored, and is in the collection of the Australian National Gallery, Canberra.

An unusual miniaturist, a wax modeller, arrived in Tasmania in 1837. This was **Theresa Susannah Eunice Snell Chauncy** (1807–1876), who met and married Lieutenant John Walker. She was a skilled modeller in wax, and exhibited at the Royal Academy of Arts in 1841. While in Tasmania she produced wax portraits of governors, clergy and businessmen. Examples of her work are held in South Australian and Tasmanian galleries.

Her sister, **Martha Maria Snell Chauncy Berkeley** (1813–*c.* 1899), came to South Australia with her husband in 1847. She was known for her miniatures and also her larger works, which now hang in the Art Gallery of South Australia.

Ada Whiting was born in 1858. She was living in Melbourne and painting miniatures in 1905, when the Art Gallery of NSW purchased one of her works for ten pounds. They were later to add two more of her portraits to their collection. At the time of writing, a small portrait of a child by Ada is for sale for $8000 in a Sydney antique shop. She exhibited portrait and wildflower studies with the Victorian Art Society during 1898 and 1916.

(Work by these early Australian artists,

where attribution can be confirmed, is very scarce, and prices have escalated since 1988, when the bi-centenary of the nation was celebrated.)

Born in Ipswich, Queensland, **Bessie Gibson** (1868–1961) studied at the Central Technical School with Godfrey Rivers. She left Brisbane in 1905 aged 37, to study in Paris. Here she studied under Mlle Debillemont-Chardon (miniatures), Colarossi and Castelucho (*c.* 1907). She painted large-format work as well as miniatures. She lived in Paris for 40 years, finally returning to Brisbane in 1947. Her work is included in various Australian gallery collections.

Stella Marks (née Lewis) was born in Victoria in 1888. She studied at the National Gallery School in Victoria with Bernard Hall and Frederick McCubbin. She later studied in London, and was a member of the Royal Miniature Society and the American Society of Miniature Painters. In later years she was commissioned to paint members of the Royal Family.

Louisa Ann Meredith had established herself as a miniaturist and writer in Birmingham, before arriving in New South Wales in 1839. She settled in Tasmania with her husband in 1840, where she was better known for her paintings of local flowers and animals.

Georgiana Huntley McCrae (1804–1890) was trained in England by John Varley, John Glover and Charles Hayter, and worked professionally before her marriage to Andrew Murison McCrae. She arrived with her husband in Victoria in 1841, bore eight children, and died in 1890. Those few portraits and miniatures she did execute remain in the family, or may exist in a few private collections as it was considered not fitting for a gentlewoman to sell her work. Some of her miniatures were

published when her journal was printed in 1934 (edited by Hugh McCrae).

Bess Norris was born in 1878 in Prahran, Victoria and studied with McCubbin at the Melbourne Gallery. She left Australia when she was 19, settled in London, and continued her studies at the Slade Art School. She received acknowledgment for her watercolour portraits, but it was her miniatures which won her greatest acclaim. She died in London in 1939. Galleries in Melbourne and Sydney have examples of her work.

Born in England, **Bernice Edwell** (1880–1962) came to Australia as a child. Later she painted in Sydney and Melbourne. She was taught at the Royal Art Society School and later at the Colarossis' Studio in Paris. While there, two of her miniatures were hung in the Salon. The National Gallery purchased one of her miniatures in 1917. The Art Gallery of NSW has four excellent examples. Two are profile studies (*c.* 1930), and are freely painted.

Georgiana McCrae (1805–1890). An unknown woman. Possibly painted early in her painting career. Watercolour on ivory/paper. Image size 5.3 cm x 4 cm (2 in x 1½ in). In the collection of the artist's family.

Creative Miniatures

Daisy M. Brookes was born in England in 1887, and came to Sydney in 1915. She worked for Fox photographic studios painting portraits and colouring photographs.

She was an exhibiting member of the Royal Society of Miniature Painters, Sculptors and Gravers, but in later years, as her eyesight was failing, she is said to have given up her position in the Society to allow room for a new member. She was still painting in 1980.

A three-quarter length miniature portrait, purchased by the Art Gallery of NSW in 1919 for 15 guineas, called 'Jeunesse', is a delightful study. In cream and grey, it shows freedom, wit and movement — something rare in miniature painting.

It is interesting, when one takes an overall view of the development of Australian miniatures, to see that the best work of the early artists, whether they were convicts or free settlers, reflected the best of English and European style at the time, and the exponents appear to be predominantly male. Though some of the work was on card, ivory was still the main support.

The later period, from about 1880 to the present time, appears to be dominated by women artists. Economic factors possibly play a large part. Miniatures, taking as they often do, at least three times as long to paint as a large easel work, have rarely provided a viable monetary return.

In works catalogued of acquisitions from 1910 by the Art Gallery of NSW, the support is listed as ivory or ivorine, showing that ivorine was an accepted support in Australia at this time.

With some of the women artists there is an obvious change in style. Some were no longer using the stipple or stroke approach but were using free watercolour washes with great effect.

Maybe, in the future, a way will be found to display these treasures again, and they will emerge from their present sleep in the subterranean storage drawers. With the ever-growing public interest in miniatures it would be wonderful to be able to see and study them.

Societies and Collections

Australia

SOCIETIES:
NSW
The Australian Society of Miniature Art
INC.
Mrs Janine Bravery, President, 142 Tryon
Road, East Lindfield NSW 2070.
Tel: (02) 416 2629.
Traditional and contemporary miniatures.
Maximum size 10 cm x 10 cm (4 in x 4 in).

Qld
The Australian Society of Miniature Art
(Qld) INC.
Mrs Marilyn Peck, President, P.O. Box
548, Mermaid Beach, Qld 4218.
Tel: (075) 332 823.
Traditional and contemporary miniatures.

CONTACTS:
Victoria
Noela Patané,
P.O. Box 383, Eltham, Vic, 3095.
Tel: (03) 431 2545.

Tasmania
Mrs Bernadette Connor,
Hibiscus Gallery, 5 Ashfield Street, Sandy
Bay, Hobart, Tas 7005. Tel: (002) 23 6001.

SPECIAL COLLECTIONS
Special arrangements must be made to
view most collections.
Mitchell Library, Macquarie St, Sydney.
Art Gallery of NSW, Sydney.
Allport Library and Museum of Fine Arts,
State Library of Tasmania, Hobart.

Queensland Art Gallery.
Australian National Gallery, Canberra.
Art Gallery of South Australia.
National Gallery of Victoria.

RETAIL COLLECTIONS OF MINIATURES
AND SILHOUETTES:
Janet Niven, 118 Queen St, Woollahra
NSW 2025. Tel: (02) 363 2211.
Member of the Antique Dealers
Association of New South Wales.

Red Hill Gallery, 61 Musgrave Rd, Red
Hill, Qld 4059. Tel: (07) 368 1442.

Competitive Exhibition

UNITED KINGDOM
The Royal Society of Miniature Painters,
Sculptors and Gravers, 17 Carlton House
Terrace, London SW1.
Traditional paintings and silhouettes.
Maximum size 17.5 cm x 12.5 cm (7 in x
5 in). Application for membership by
submission of work in the manner
requested by the society.

CANADA
Annual International Competitive
Exhibition, Del Bello Gallery, 363 Queen
Street West, Toronto, Ontario M5V 2A4.
Tel: (416) 593 0884.
Entry forms June–July, Exhibition
November–December. Traditional and
Contemporary. Maximum size 7.5 cm x
10 cm (3 in x 4 in).

Suppliers

All large art suppliers will keep watercolour papers, pastellist's paper, paints and brushes.

Australia

Ivorine, vellum, gold leaf and other art supplies:
Will's Quills,
164 Victoria Ave, Chatswood NSW 2067.
Tel: (02) 419 6031.

Robel Framing Gallery,
73-75 Mackie Road, Mulgrave, Vic 3170.
Tel: (03) 561 7111.

Miniaturists' painting box with easel, palette, ivorine and other art supplies:
Peninsula Plaza Art Supplies,
20 Bungan St, Mona Vale NSW 2103.
Tel: (02) 979 6559.

English and French scraperboard, ivorine and other art supplies:
Janet's Art Supplies,
145 Victoria Ave, Chatswood NSW 2067.
Tel: (02) 417 6048.

Schmincke watercolours and other art supplies:
The Art Scene,
914 Victoria Rd, West Ryde NSW 2114.
Tel: (02) 807 6440.

J. Walch & Sons Pty Ltd,
130 Macquarie St, Hobart, Tas 7000.
Tel: (002) 23 3444.

Conservator and Jeweller

Karen Coote, B.A. (Sydney),
B.Sc. (London), trained jeweller and archaeological conservator. Tel: (02) 810 5335 for enquiries regarding care of miniatures.

United Kingdom

Plated gold frames (oval) specifically for the miniaturist:
R. J. W. Products,
1 Georgian Close, Hayes, Bromley, Kent BR2 7RA.
L. Cornelissen & Son,
105 Great Russell St, London WC1 BRY.
Tel: (01) 636 1046.

Acknowledgments

It has been a great pleasure to write these notes and I would like to thank Simon & Schuster for making it possible.

I would like to thank all my students, both past and present, who have assisted in so many ways, gathering information, making suggestions and proofreading early manuscript sheets. In particular, I would like to thank Gerardine Stanley, student and later exhibiting member, and secretary of the Australian Society of Miniature Art; Sally Coffey, artist and friend, who obtained in London volumes not available in Australia, which provided valuable research material; Gloria Allport, artist and Kuring-gai Art Centre manager for support and encouragement; my past teachers, whose voices I hear when I work; Henry Gibbons (deceased) (Julian Ashton Art School); Professor Joe Klimek (Seaforth Technical College); Terry Swann; Judy Lane; Ian Chapman; Mr Brian Caldersmith, who finally taught me (by proxy) how to draw a triangle in a circle; kind custodians who allowed me to photograph their private collections, including M. Kinsman, A. Carney, L. Roget, Dr R. Bligh, and J. Niven; Elizabeth Imashev, Curator of Paintings, Mitchell Library, State Library of NSW, for her assistance with resource avenues for the Australian History section; Karen Coote, jeweller and archaeological conservator for her time; and finally, all those artists who agreed so willingly to have their work included, and those who prepared work for 'step-by-step' segments.

I have relied heavily on the Australian portrait research of Eve Buscombe, to extract those early artists who were also miniaturists, and on the work of Murdoch, Murrell, Noon and Strong for technical methods of early miniaturists.

To all, I am sincerely grateful.

Photographs on pages 16, 39, 60, 62 (top), 79–80, 82–3 by Jonathan Chester. Photographs on pages 40, 43, 44, 64, 86 and 87 by Geoff Hirst. All other photographs by Patricia Moy.

Bibliography

Alexander, J. J. G., *The Decorated Letter*, Thames and Hudson (London), 1978.

Angel, Marie, *Painting for Calligraphers*, Pelham Books (London), 1984.

Burke, Janine, *Australian Women Artists 1840–1940*, Greenhouse Publications (Melbourne), 1980.

Buscombe, Eve, *Artists in Early Australia and Their Portraits*, The Power Institute of Fine Arts, University of Sydney, Eureka Research (Sydney), 1978.

—, *Australian Colonial Portraits, Exhibition Catalogue*, researched & selected Tasmanian Art Gallery & Museum, 1979.

Campbell, Jean, *Australian Watercolour Painting*, Craftsman House (Sydney), 1989.

Cobley, John, Dr, *Sydney Cove 1788, Original Diaries*, Edited, Hodder & Stoughton (U.K.), 1962.

Cook, Peter, *The Antique Buyers Handbook 2*, Reed (Sydney), 1982.

Dalley, Terence (Editor), *The Complete Guide to Illustration and Design*, QED (London), 1980.

Douglas, Phoebe Sholto, *Painting in Miniature*, Magazine Series-Artist (England), 1983.

Foskett, Daphne, *British Portrait Miniatures*, University Press (Glasgow), 1963.

Flower, Cedric, *Duck and Cabbage Tree*, arranged and annotated, Angus & Robertson (Sydney), 1968.

Heller, Jules, *Printmaking Today*, Holt, Rineheart and Winston, Inc. (U.S.A.), 1972.

Hooper, Juliana & Toby, *A Guide to Collecting Australiana*, Macmillan (Australia), 1978.

Jackson, Donald, *The Story of Writing*, Studio Vista in Association with Parker Pen (U.K.), 1981.

Jones, Shar, *Early Painters of Australia*, Bay Books (Sydney), 1988.

Kerr, Joan, *Dictionary of Australian Artists, Working Paper 1770–1870 A–H*, Power Institute of Fine Arts, University of Sydney, 1984.

Kronsky, Betty, 'The Psychology of Art', *American Artist*, Magazine, July, 1984.

Loftie, W. J., *Lessons in the Art of Illuminating*, Blackie & Son (London) (date unknown).

Mayer, Ralph, *The Artist's Handbook of Materials and Techniques*, Faber & Faber (U.K.), 1951.

Moore, William, *The Story of Australian Art Vol 1*, Angus & Robertson (Sydney), 1934.

Moorehead, Alan, *Cooper's Creek*, Hamish Hamilton Ltd (U.K.), 1963.

McCormick, Tim, *First Views of Australia 1788–1825*, David Ell Press Longueville Publications (Sydney), 1987.

McCulloch, Alan, *Encyclopedia of Australian Art*, Hutchison Group Australia, 1984.

Murdoch, Murrell, Noon & Strong, *The English Miniature*, Yale University Press (New Haven & London), 1981.

Ramsey, L. G. G. (Editor), *The Complete Encyclopaedia of Antiques*, Richard Clay & Co. Ltd (London), 1962.

Reynolds, Graham, *Wallace Collection — Catalogue of Miniatures*, Catalogue, the Trustees of the Wallace Collection (London), 1980.

Royal Society of Miniature Painters, Sculptors and Gravers, *90th Exhibition*, Catalogue, the Trustees (London), 1988.

Sotheby's, *Objects of Vertu, Fans, Portrait Miniatures and Silver Smallwork*, Catalogue (London), March 1985.

Strong, Roy, *Artists of the Tudor Court*, Catalogue, Victoria & Albert Museum (London), 1983.

The Tate Gallery & Winsor & Newton Exhibition, Paint & Painting Catalogue, the Trustees (London), 1982.

Thomas, Daniel, (Editor), *Creating Australia*, Catalogue, Art Gallery of South Australia (Adelaide), 1988.

Thornton, R. K. J. and Cain, T. G. S., (Editors), *A Treatise Concerning the Art of Limning* by Nicholas Hillard (Ashington:mid-Northumberland Arts Group in association with Carcanet New Press), 1981.

Willies, Joan, *The Artist's Workbook on Miniature Painting*, privately printed (Florida), 1988.

Glossary

Daguerreotype   A method of making and fixing a photographic image. Invented by L. J. M. Daguerre in 1833.

Gesso   Traditionally a chalk-glue mixture, fully absorbent and used in tempera painting and water gilding. Gesso referred to in this book is *polymer gesso* which is non-absorbent. Used for coating canvas and board when a non-absorbent surface is required.

Gouache   Opaque watercolour usually sold in tubes. In this book when reference is made to *gouache* it is the addition of white to artist's watercolour by the artist as opacity is required.

Gum amoniac   A resinous gum which is soaked, strained and used for laying gold leaf in the traditional manner.

Ivorine   A thin, translucent, plastic-like material used by miniaturists as a substitute for ivory.

Ivory   Used in thin, translucent sheets as a support for painting by miniaturists. Generally obtained from the tusks of elephants.

Parchment and vellum   Made from the skin of calves, goats and sheep. The finest grades are made from the skins of newborn animals. Used by early miniaturists as a support and still in use today.

Silverpoint   Pure silver used to draw on a specially prepared ground or base. Metal point (silver and gold) was used for drawing prior to the manufacture of pencils using graphite and wood.

Sized   Paper which has been hardened with animal glue or gelatine, by passing the finished sheet through a bath of glue.

Support   In this book refers to the base used for the painting, for example, vellum, ivory, ivorine, mat board, wood and paper.

INDEX

Index